SHIPRA

India and Central Asia

India and Central Asia
(Cultural, Economic and Political Links)

Editor
Surendra Gopal

SHIPRA

Maulana Abul Kalam Azad Institute of Asian Studies, Calcutta

ISBN : 81-7541-072-8

First Published in India in 2001

India and Central Asia

© Maulana Abul Kalam Azad Institute of Asian Studies

Published by :
SHIPRA PUBLICATIONS
115-A, Vikas Marg, Shakarpur,
Delhi-110092 (India)
Ph : 2458662, 2200954 Fax : 91-11-2458662
Email : siprapub@satyam.net.in

Laser Typeset by :
Sunshine Graphics
Delhi-110032

Printed at :
Chaudhary Offset Process
Delhi-110051

Preface

The present volume consisting of seven essays by four scholars, two each from India and Russia, focusses on India's close relationship with Central Asia from the medieval times to the early decades of the 20th century. Being neighbours, there has been a regular flow of men and merchandise between the two regions since antiquity. In fact, cultural interaction and economic intercourse between India and Central Asia can be traced as far back as the end of the third and beginning of the second millennium B.C. The relics of the Altyn-Tepe culture testify to the existence of close ties between the towns and settlements of South Turkmenistan of the Indus Valley in Sind (Harappa and Mohenjodaro) and similar types of sites excavated on the Gujarat coast and in Rajasthan along the now-extinct river Saraswati, reaching further east to a part of the Gangetic plain and Western Uttar Pradesh. The Indo-Central Asian ties are thus much older than the first migration of the Turkic tribes to Central Asia and the advent of Islam in that region.

These contacts became closer during the period of the Achaemenid empire and Alexander the Great when regions of Central Asia like Bactria, Sogd, Parthia and Khwarezm became parts of a common state together with such territories of North-West India as the Gandhara region and the Indus valley. During the Kushan period relations between India and Central Asia reached their zenith. The Kushan epoch was a time of great enrichment of cultures of India and Central Asia through their synthesis. The Kushan coins bear witness to the co-existence zoroastrianism with the Indian religions of Buddhism and Saivism. During this period the two regions flourished materially due to the operation of the Great Silk Route connecting China and the Far East with Europe and India through Central Asia.

The cultural and economic interaction between India and Central Asia continued albeit on a smaller scale, in the post-Kushan period. The excavations at Penjikent (Tajikistan), Varaksha (Uzbekistan) and Adzhina-Tepe (Tajikistan) brought to light frescoes reminiscent of Bharhut and Ajanta caves in India. At Penjikent a fresco carries the painting of a blue dancer wearing tiger skin and with a trident in the background has been identified with the legend of the Indian god Siva becoming *nilkantha* (blue necked). At Varaksha a painting on the palace wall showing the king hunting a tiger riding on elephant back along with his retinue is clearly influenced by Indian tradition. The most striking find is, however, from Adzhina-Tepe. It is the figure of sleeping Buddha in the *nirvana* posture (size about 12 metres). A number of Buddhist Sanskrit manuscripts have been discovered in excavations at Zang-Tepe near Termez in Uzbekistan. A Sanskrit language Buddhist text of 300 sheets of palm leaves dating from 7th century A.D. discovered from a place near Merv in Turkmenistan has been identified as *Vinayapitaka*.

The political and socio-cultural links which were forged between India and Central Asia in ancient times persisted and further developed during the medieval period. The friendly visits of scholars from Khwarezm—Al-Beruni and Abdurazzak Samarkandi—form a glorious chapter in the history of contacts between India and Central Asia. Some of the Delhi Sultans who ruled before the founding of the Mughal Empire by Babar were scions of the Turkmen tribes Khilji and Tughlak. Bairam Khan, the tutor-guardian of the Mughal Emperor Akbar, was a Turkmen. His son Abdul Rahim Khan-e-Khana was an eminent poet who also wrote verses in Hindi. Works of Indian scholars like Aryabhatta on astronomy and mathematics and of Charak and Susrut on medicine were known to Central Asian scholars Al-Khwarezmi and Ibn-e-Sina through their Arabic translations.

Many Muslim Sufi saints came to India from the Central Asian cities of Bukhara and Samarkand. According to Akbar's historian Abdul Fazl, poets from Bukhara and Merv stayed at the imperial court and a number of high-ranking nobles (*mansabdars*) were of

Central Asian origin. Sugar, cotton and silk cloth, indigo and spices figured prominently among the commodities exported to Central Asia from India where imported Central Asian horses, dry fruits and precious stones were in great demand. Melons and grapes from Samarkand came regularly to India in abundant quantity during the reins of Akbar and Jehangir. A family of architects from Khojent (Tajikistan) was associated with a number of Mughal buildings. According to the author of *Tьʌikh-e-Mubarak Shahi* affluent Central Asian merchants used to send books among other articles for sale in their region.

The socio-cultural, political and economic contacts between India and Central Asia in modern times form a field of study no less fascinating than their development in earlier ancient and medieval periods. However, no full-fledged studies of these close links with Central Asia have been conducted so far in India barring one or two relating to the ancient and modern times. The studies published in India in the form of research articles and occasional papers have largely remained confined to such themes as migration of the Aryans and various other tribes, the spread of Buddhism and the development of Kushan art, the impact of Central Asia on the art and architecture of India in the medieval period and the origins of various mystic Sufi sects.

Soviet Russian and Central Asian scholars have written profusely on Indo-Central Asian contacts using the vast primary source material including the archival, available in Russian and Central Asian languages in the libraries and archives of Tashkent, Moscow and St. Petersburg. The publication in Moscow in 1958 of a collection of documents throwing light on the Russo-Indian relations during the seventeenth century enabled historians to write on the role of Indian traders in Central Asia in the Russo-Indian relations. In 1964 N.B. Baikova published from Tashkent a research monograph *Rol' Srednei Azii v Russko-Indiiskikh Torgovykh Svyazakh* (Role of Central Asia in Russo-Indian Trade Relations). Baikova in her monograph highlighted Central Asia as a connecting link in the Russo-Indian trade from the first half of the sixteenth to the second half of the eighteenth century. There existed in Astrakhan since 1630s a colony of Indian merchants. Astrakhan is located at the place where the Volga river falls into the Caspian Sea the coast of which is shared by Russia with Iran. In the beginning Russia tried to develop its trade with India through Iran. But the long distance involved and the political uncertainties in that country drove her to develop Orenburg on the Ural river as a base for trade with India via Central Asia. Baikova's work brought out the fact that the Central Asian market was the main attraction for Indian traders and their interest in the Russian market was a by-product of their trade with Iran and Central Asia. The publication in 1965 of another volume containing documents on Russo-Indian relations during the eighteenth century provided new data and rich material showing the increasing trade links of Central Asia with India.

In all, the book contains seven essays. The three essays by Surendra Gopal throw light on Indians in Central Asia during the 16th and 17th centuries and outline the activities of Indian traders on the territory of present-day Uzbekistan in the eighteenth century as also on the Pamir plateau in the first decade of the nineteenth century. The two essays by Devendra Kaushik deal respectively with the economic relations between India and Central Asia during the nineteenth century and reconstruct the history of political contacts between the two regions from the colonial period to the aftermath of the Socialist Revolution. The other two essays by Russian scholars, late G.L. Dmitriyev from Tashkent and late I.M. Oranskii from Leningrad (St. Petersburg) give respectively a socio-cultural profile of the Indian settlers in Central Asia during the latter half of the nineteenth and early twentieth century and information about an ethno-linguistic group of Indians called *pariah* settled in parts of Tajikistan and Uzbekistan. These two essays by Russian scholars have been translated from Russian.

As borne out by facts emanating from several contributions to the present volume, the ties between India and Central Asia were never totally disrupted notwithstanding the inhibiting effect of Anglo-Russian colonial rivalry. Ruminating over the past one gets more and more convinced about the organic linkages between geoculture and geopolitics and geoeconomics. Frequent closures of the route through Afghanistan on account of inter-tribal conflicts and wars of succession did not dampen the spirit of the Indian traders who switched over to trade through Persia before settling down in the 90s of the 19th century in favour of the Bombay-Batumi sea route and thence by rail to the Caspian and across the Caspian to the port of Krasnovodsk in Central Asia. This sea and rail route to Central Asia became popular because of reduced cost of transport. The fact that before appearance of the geopolitical perspective, the peoples of both the regions had been drawn close to each other due to the millennia-old cultural contacts based on their inclusion in a common cultural complex imparted strength to them for overcoming the political barriers.

The editor would like to acknowledge the financial support of the Maulana Abul Kalam Azad Institute of Asian Studies, Calcutta, which enabled him to see through the publication of this volume as part of a project taken up as a Fellow of the Institute. I also extend my sincere thanks to Prof. Devendra Kaushik, Chairman of the Executive Council of the Institute, for contributing two scholarly papers to the volume and for arranging to provide the other two papers of Russain scholars for inclusion in it.

It is hoped this little volume will contribute its mite to the further strengthening of the age-old traditional historico-cultural and economic bonds between India and Central Asia. The archives and libraries of undivided India and the former Soviet Union contain a wealth of material as yet untapped for reconstructing the grand saga of multifaceted interaction between the peoples of India and Central Asia. If the present collection could provide a stimulus to historians to produce a comprehensive work on the subject, the editor will feel more than gratified.

Surendra Gopal

Contents

Contents

Abbreviations

AVPR	Arkhiv Vneshnyi Politiki Rossii
IHC	Indian History Congress
L	Leningrad (now Peterburg)
LGU	Leningradskii Gosudarstvennoi Universitet
M	Moscow
R-I.O. v XVII V.	Russko-Indiiskiye Otnosheniya v XVII Veke
R-I.O. v XVIII V.	Russko-Indiiskiye Otnosheniya v XVIII V.
Ts G A Uz SSR	Tsentralnyi Gosudarstvennyi Arkhiv Uzbekistan SSR
Ts G A SSSR	Tsentralnyi Gosudarstvenyi Arkhiv, SSSR
Ts G V I SSSR	Tsentralny Gosudarstvenyi Vneshnii Istoricheskii Arkhiv SSSR
NAI	National Archives of India
SPB	St. Peterburg/Petersburg

Abbreviations used in Russian archival sources (not in alphabetical order)

F.	Fond (Fund/ Main Collection/ Holding)
op.	Opis (Inventory/ Schedule)
d.	Delo (File)
L.	Listya(Sheet/ Folio/ Page)

Indians in Central Asia
16th and 17th Centuries*

Surendra Gopal

Trade involves transfer of goods from one part of the world to
another and ensures interaction between two peoples. Thanks to
researchers, both Indian and non-Indian, especially in the post-
independence period, we have a fairly comprehensive idea of the
flow of goods and men, indigenous and foreign and the various
regions in our country as well as abroad which participated in this
exchange. Absence of statistical data prevents us from determining
the volume and value of goods exchanged. Besides, we have only
the haziest of ideas of the activities of our countrymen who had
reached foreign lands after sailing across high seas, or crossing
snowy mountains and inhospitable deserts and steppes. Our efforts
should now be directed towards delineating the activities of our
countrymen abroad. This is a formidable task: the area of their
operations was vast. It roughly ranged from the east coast of Africa
to the Indonesian archipelago.[1] It also includes countries in the
heart of the Asian mainland, the fertile crescent, the Iranian cities,
the Caucasus region, the Russian and the Central Asian steppes,
Tibet, etc.

---

* *Proceedings*, Indian History Congress, 52nd Session, New Delhi,
   1992 pp.219-31.

1

When Vasco da Gama reached the shores of East Africa in 1498 he found Indians there. In the ports on the Red Sea and in the interior of the Arabian peninsula also the Indian presence was noteworthy. In Persia, Olearius estimated the number of Indians to be 12,000.[2] Among them were several non-Muslims, known as Multanis,[3] who applied yellow colour on their forehead and cremated their dead. In the South-east Asia, the Europeans found resident Indians. If we focus our researches on the activities of our countrymen abroad during the Mughal period we will be adding to the knowledge of the history of our people.

This is a difficult work; data are scanty and scattered. Our Persian chronicles, the most important source of Mughal history, are hardly of any help. Our countrymen who journeyed abroad have left practically no accounts of these visits. We are basically dependent for our study on the writings of non-Indians. But even they are not prolific; they noted the presence of Indians only in passing. Part of the reason for their brevity could be that in the Islamic countries, the identity of Indian Muslims was submerged either in the local Muslim population or in the Muslim traders of the other countries.

I

By middle Central Asia, we mean the region described in contemporary literature as *Mawarannahar* or Transoxiana, roughly lying east of the Caspian Sea, north of the Amu or Oxus river (including the region of Balkh), west of Badakhshan and south of the Syr Darya or the Jaxartes river.

India's contacts with Central Asia or Transoxiana go back to antiquity and there has been exchange of population at different levels; traders, scholars, religious preachers, job-seekers, etc., have been crossing the boundaries of the two areas in spite of changes in the political boundaries and political climate. The travel was certainly facilitated by large number of available entry points from Kashmir in the north to Sindh in the south on our north-western boundary. Abul Fazl speaks of seven routes frequented between Afghanistan and Transoxiana.[4] Akbar had made the journey to Kabul, an important departure point for Indians intending to go to Central Asia, easier by making the road across the Khyber pass fit for vehicular traffic.[5]

Mir Izzatollah in the beginning of the nineteenth century spoke of twenty-two routes and a couple of decades later Mohanlal quoted the number at forty.[6] Besides one could cross to Yarkand and Kashgar from north Kashmir and then turn westwards to the Farghana valley and thereafter to Tashkent or the Kazakh steppes. But for going to Central Asia, Kabul and Kandhar had emerged as the two most popular exit points.[7]

The contacts between India and Central Asia, became long-ranging and regular when the Islamized Central Asian Turks established their control over north India in the early thirteenth century. The Mongol invasions may have temporarily disrupted the traffic but Timur's incorporation of a part of north western India into his empire restored the old intensity in the relationship between the two regions. Timur's close diplomatic ties[8] with China ensured that Indians could not only move up to Black Sea in the west but also visit the Chinese empire.

Timur, after his conquest of Delhi, handed over a large number of skilled craftsmen to princes, nobles and other members of his entourage. Some of these Indians were taken to Samarkand. Timur ordered that stone-masons should be reserved for his own use as he wanted to construct a mosque in Samarkand.[9] Indians formed a segment of the population of the city. Babur also found on the banks of river Baran, a colony of three hundred families of slaves, who had been brought and settled from the suburb of Multan to catch birds and fish by a member of Timur's family.[10]

Timur and his successors had transformed Samarkand into the premier trading mart of Central Asia by establishing close contacts with European nations and China. Timur wrote letters to the rulers of France and England and explicitly stated that the traders were welcome and would face no hindrance in their activities.[11] A Spanish visitor to Timur's court during 1403-1406 wrote that Samarkand was full of goods from different countries; from India came the finest of spices, such as 'the best variety of nutmegs, cloves, mace, ginger, etc.'.[12] Between 1403 and 1409 Samarkand sent thirty-three diplomatic missions to China. During the same period China received fourteen embassies from Herat, besides three diplomatic missions from Badakhshan, two from Andhoya (!) and one each from Khojent, Andijan and Margdine.[13]

Shah Rukh, the ruler of Herat (1409-1447) sent his envoy Abdur Razzak to the king of Vijaynagar where he stayed from 1442 to 1444.[14] The Russian trader Afanasi Nikitin also visited the courts of Bahmani Sultans a quarter of century later (1469-72 or 1472-74), having reached India by the sea-route from Persia.[15]

Hence, by the beginning of the fifteenth century, a very congenial situation prevailed for the overall growth of trade in the entire region. Indians took advantage of new economic opportunities. However, we are as yet, in no position to describe it in quantitative terms but a source lamenting the change brought by the arrival of the Portuguese in the Indian ports in 1498 says that the disruption of Indian sea trade with Persia had caused a spurt in the caravan trade.[16] It is against this background that we should evaluate the statement of Babur made in 1505 that every year 'ten, fifteen to twenty thousand Indian merchants' arrived in Kabul with slaves, sugar, white cloth and medicinal herbs.[17] We do not know how many of them travelled to Iran or Central Asia or to Tibet and China but certainly some of them did move to Transoxiana. He had also noted that caravans came to Kabul from Farghana, Turkestan, Samarkand, Bukhara, Balkh, Hisar and Badakhshan.[18] The merchants remained unhappy even when they made a profit of 300 or 400 per cent.[19]

II

Babur, driven out of his paternal kingdom by the Shaibanids, settled down in Kabul and in 1526 succeeded in establishing his dynasty in India. He was always nostalgic about his homeland and the lost principality of Samarkand. The Shaibanids, despite all animosities did not shun diplomatic contacts. In 1528-29 an Uzbek embassy consisting of Khoja Kalan, Abdul Shahid and a member of the House of Shaibanids visited him.[20] That people could cross the frontiers in large groups is also evident from Jauhar's statement that five hundred Mughal soldiers from across the Oxus river seeking employment with Humayun entered Kabul.[21]

It can safely be presumed that the number of Indian visitors to the Central Asian markets increased since the political changes around the Caspian Sea had further broadened economic contacts of the region. The Russian Tsar, Ivan III had brought the Khanate of Kazan under his vassalage in 1487 and gradually the Russian arms were moving towards Astrakhan in order to ensure for the Russians unhindered access to the Caspian Sea through the Volga river. The Bukharans who had emerged as an important power were keen to exploit this opportunity and had sent a caravan to Astrakhan in 1537.[22] In 1552 the Russian Tsar occupied Kazan and the Russians could easily reach the Caspian Sea. In the fifties the Tsar permitted an Englishman, Anthony Jenkinson to sail over the Caspian Sea and the Englishman arrived in Bukhara in 1558. Jenkinson reporting on the trade of the place noted, "There is yearly great resort of Merchants to this Cities of Boghar, which travel in great caravans from the countries there about adjoining as India, Persia, Balkh, Russia with diverse others, ...The chief commodities that are brought thither out of these aforesaid countries, are the following:

The Indians doe bring fine whites, which the Tartars doe all roll about their heads, and all other kindes of whites, which serve for apparell made of cotton wool and Crasca, but Gold, Silver, precious stones and spices they bring none... .the Indian carry from Boghar against wrought Silkes, red hides, slaves and horses, with such like... I offered to barter with merchants of those countries, which came from the farthest parts of India, even from the Countrey of Bengala, and the river, Ganges, to give them Kerseis for their commodities but they would not barter for such commodities as Cloath"[23]

Jenkinson realized the hazards of such a long journey. He noted that even though a caravan from India had been assured safety by the rulers it had been robbed, 'a great part slaine', at about 'ten days journey from Boghar' by 'theaves'.[24]

Almost four decades later, the picture had not materially altered. Badruddin Kashmiri, a contemporary author speaks of Central Asians who possessed goods looted from the caravan of traders.[25] Insecurity on the roads was a strong deterrent yet the Mughal occupation and hold over Afghanistan enabled Indians to move to Central Asia from Kandhar, Kabul or Kashmir in the sixteenth century with comparative security.

The Central Asian exports to India were silk and half-silk textiles, crimson velvet, carpets, bronze and copper utensils, arms such as sabres, knives, shields, armours, Bukharan bows, etc., and a variety of fresh fruits such as apples, melons, quinces, grapes, etc., and dried fruits such as almonds, pistachios, raisins, etc. The Samarkand paper (both Sultani and Miribrahimi) enjoyed great demand in India. Samarkand also sent to India horses and camels besides Russian goods.[26] Babur had also spoken of the export of dry fruits from Central Asia to India.

III

The demand for Central Asian horses never slackened in India because of their large-scale deployment on the battle-fields and their use for quick transport from place to place. Babur noted that every year in Kabul arrived, 'seven, eight or ten thousand horses'.[27] Bernier, the French traveller (1658-67) put the figure at twenty-five thousand annually.[28] Towards the end of the seventeenth century, Manucci stated that Indian traders purchased horses of Balkh and Bukhara at Kabul numbering 1,00,000.[29] According to a fourteenth century source the profit in this trade was estimated at 2500 per cent.[30] The trade in horses was considerable, both in terms of number as well as value. The Indian merchants did participate in it in the seventeenth century as they had done in the sixteenth century as pointed out by Jenkinson.

As stated earlier, India received a large supply of dry fruits from the region, and Bernier noted the sale of dry fruits from 'Persia, Balkh, Bukhara and Samarkand' in the markets of Delhi.[31] Under Jahangir a new dimension was added and India started receiving fresh fruits from the region. The export of fresh fruits from the Central Asia received a great boost after Jahangir's accession to the throne since he loved them immensely. He received melons grown in Kariz near Herat, grapes and apples from Samarkand.[32] He boasts that although his father Akbar was a great lover of melons, pomegranates and grapes, yet "during his time the Kariz melons, which are the finest kind, and pomegranates from Yezd, which are celebrated throughout the world and Samarkand grapes had never been brought to Hindustan".[33] On receiving another consignment of Kariz melons, he writes, "Although this is at a distance of 1400 kos, and kaphilas take five months to come, they arrived very ripe and fresh. They brought so many that they sufficed for all the servants".[34] While staying at Ahmedabad, he received 1500 melons from Kariz.[35]

Bernier also noted the sale of 'fresh grapes, black and white, brought from (Persia, Bulkh, Bukhara and Samarkand), wrapped in cotton; pears and apples of three or four sorts and those admirable melons which last the whole winter. These fruits are however, very dear...'.[36] Bernier had no hesitation in saying, "Usbec being the country which principally supplies Delhi with these (fresh and dry) fruits, which are eaten all the winter,...'.[37] He commented, "...Hindustan consumes an immense quantity of fresh fruit from Samarkand, (Balkh), Bocara and Persia,...".

When Abdullah Khan II conquered Badakhshan (1584), Herat (1588) and Khorezm (1593-94), political stability was imparted to Central Asia. Akbar had cordial relations with him as is evident from the exchange of a number of embassies between them. Indians enjoyed easier access to Central Asia.[38]

Abdullah Khan, proclaimed himself Khan of Turan in 1583 and Hindukush became the boundary between the Uzbeks and the Mughals.[39] The Indians were now a segment of the local population in Samarkand as is evident from the collection of sixteenth century documents from the office of the Qazi of Samarkand "Majmua' i-Vasaik" discovered by R.G. Mukminova.

A document describes Daria Khan Multani, son of Shaikh Sadi as a very rich merchant of Samarkand. He is mentioned in eight documents bearing the seal of the Qazi of Samarkand, dated either A.D. 1589 or A.D. 1590. No other individual is referred to in so many documents.

A document dated 13 October 1589 writes about Lahori Chittar son of Laly who had promised to pay Daria Khan Multani a sum of one hundred and fifty *tangas* as and when asked.[40]

In another document executed on the same day, Lahori Chittar undertook not to leave the place without the prior permission of Daria Khan. He also divorced his wife by uttering the word *talaq* three times.

In another document of 25 November 1589 Mullah Hussain, son of Painda Multani promised to deliver to Daria Khan thirty-two pieces of cloth 'Chit-i-Purband' measuring 12 x 1 'gaj Mukassar' within four months.[41]

On 19 September 1590, Ustad Gazor Multani, son of Ustad Hussain Multani executed a document in which he confessed that he owed to Daria Khan twenty-eight silver *tangas* and seven pieces of 'purband' clothes. He undertook to return them to Daria Khan.[42]

In another document executed on 25 October 1590 we find one Mangui Gazor Multani promising to supply to Daria Khan Multani seven pieces of 'purband' textiles, each 12 'Shariat gaj' long.[43] From another document registered on 22 November 1590 we learn that Ustad Hussain, son of Pirman promised to bring to Daria Khan ninety pieces of red *chit (purband)* measuring 12 x 1 'gaj mukassar' within seven months. As a security he sent to Daria Khan, his slave, a Hindu, around twenty-seven years old. The slave was to be returned once Ustad Hussain had fulfilled his obligations.[44]

These documents make it clear that towards the end of the sixteenth century, Indian traders and craftsmen were settled in Samarkand. Daria Khan was apparently one of the richest and most influential traders. Several craftsmen were indebted to him and worked for him. Not all of them belonged to Multan, as one of them bears the surname Lahori, *i.e.*, belonging to Lahore.

The affluence of some of the Indian traders is confirmed by the fact that another Multani, Khoja Ibrahim Multani, son of Abdullah Multani owned at Samarkand a building and some residential houses.[45]

These documents belonging to the office of the Qazi frequently refer to Hindus and Afghans. Most of the non-Muslim foreigners were primarily moneylenders because the law of Shariat prohibited moneylending by the Muslims.[46]

Daria Khan is referred to in some of the documents as 'janab' or Lord. He could certainly dictate his terms to those with whom he did business. He was not only a merchant of textiles but he also dealt in other items such as in extremely fine variety of wool, used for manufacturing shawls of the Kashmir variety.[47]

These Kashmiri shawls had become well-known in Central Asia because they were sent as gifts to Zubairi Sheikhs, who were regarded as spiritual teachers by the Mughals.[48]

The Indian traders from their bases in Central Asian cities had extended their activities to the cities of Iran, cis-Syr Darya region in the north, with the Kazakhstan steppes, and even with Siberia.[49] They also had trade relations with China.[50]

For the convenience of foreign traders, caravan serais existed in several places. In Tashkent and Bukhara, there were special caravan serais for Hindu traders from India.[51]

Among Indians in Central Asia, another group which was numerous, consisted of slaves. They reached there in a number of ways. Some of them had been secured on the banks of Indus, as Father Menserrate tells us, in exchange for horses. Some of them had been taken as prisoners during the wars,[52] while others had been captured during raids on trading caravans.

These slaves were both Hindus and Muslims. Some of them were skilled craftsmen. Indian slaves with specialized skills were much sought after. Badruddin Kashmiri, the author of the manuscript, "Rauzat-ur Rizawan va hadikat al-gilman" written at the behest of the Zubairi Sheikh Khoja Sa 'ada in the reign of Abdullah Khan II informs us that four skilled stone-masons were brought from India to work on royal buildings.[53]

A document of 1590 tells us that a Hindu slave around 30 years of age was manumitted after he paid 147 silver *tangas*. He was thereafter neither to be sold nor handed over into slavery.[54]

A couple, both slaves, were set free by their master on the intervention of Mulla Painda (a Multani). However, they were required to pay him 130 *tangas* and to work for him for an year on the condition that he fed and clothed them.[55]

Abdul Abbas Muhammad Talib, the author of *Matlab at Talbin* also speaks of Indian slaves. According to him a Zubairi Khoja owned thousands of slaves, Russians, Kalmyks and Hindus, etc., who worked in fields, looked after cattle or constructed buildings.[56]

The members of the family of Zubairi Khojas and other Naqshbandi orders off and on visited the Mughal emperor Jahangir and received sumptuous gifts. In his 8th regnal year he presented Rs. 12,000/- to Khwaja Qasim brother of Khwaja Abdul Aziz, a Naqshbandi Khwaja.[57] In the the twelfth regnal year he presented a robe of honour and Rs. 5,000 to Muhsin Khwaja of Naqshbandi order from Transoxiana.[58] In the thirteenth regnal year he was so happy to receive a walrus teeth from Khwaja Hasan Zubairi that he decided to send him choicest goods worth Rs. 30,000 through Mir Baraka Bukhari as a mark of his thankfulness.[59] The Zubairi Khwajas were sent by the ruler of Turan on important missions to Shah Abbas I in Persia and Jahangir in India.[60]

The exchange of envoys continued in the time of Shahjahan.[61]

IV

In the seventeenth century, it appears that the number of Indians arriving in Central Asia increased further. One reason was Mughal control over Kabul and their ability to hold on to Kandahar for a long period and their cordial relations with the Iranian and Central Asian rulers. Jahangir boasted that he had not forgotten the Turkish language.[62] Another factor which contributed to increased flow of Indians to Central Asia was the emergence of Astrakhan on the mouth of the Volga river where it falls into the Caspian Sea as the Russian trade window to Iran and Central Asia. Furthermore, 'the wars in seas around India' while diminishing the maritime Indo-Persian trade also resulted in a spurt of caravan trade on the northwest frontier of India. Robert Steel in 1615 noted that because of dispute over the island of Ormuz between the Portuguese and the Persians, the number of camels reaching Kandahar had increased to 'twelve or fourteen thousand whereas heretofore scarcely passed three thousand....'[63] Niels Steensgaard estimates that in 1639, even after the Dutch and the British had intervened in the Indian Ocean trade, 25-30,000 camel loads of cotton material was imported annually by Persia from India.[64] Since from Kandahar a fairly convenient route ran to Central Asia, it would be a permissible guess that part of this merchandise was carried into Central Asia by Indian merchants.

Gradually Indian traders from Iran moved to Astrakhan and made it a base for their activities in Russia. Indian traders, especially from Bukhara now decided to participate in it. They were in good company since the Bukharan traders had a history of visiting Astrakhan. From Astrakhan the Indian traders moved into the heartland of Russia and appeared for the first time in Moscow in 1638.[65]

The Indian traders in Bukhara found the trade with Astrakhan more attractive as the Russian Tsars tried to establish Russo-Indian trade links from Astrakhan via Bukhara. The strong presence of Indian traders in Bukhara is attested to by the fact that under the rule of Imam Kuli Khan, a full sector of the city was occupied by Indian (Hindu) traders, who had their own chief.[66]

They were also engaged in moneylending.[67] These merchants faced all the problems, a common citizen has to endure.

Once, thieves stole a small box containing precious stones belonging to Indians from the serai in which they were staying. They, roused by the hurrying steps of the thieves, ran after them shouting in the streets. A night patrol, hearing their cries held the thieves but the thieves, by addressing one another by the name of the ruler (as the ruler was in the habit of occasionally walking in the streets in disguise) deceived the patrol and managed to flee. When next day the Indians complained to the ruler Imam Kuli Khan against the patrol, he investigated the matter and eventually restored to them the small box with precious stones.[68]

Under Shahjahan, there was an attempt by the Mughal ruler to interfere in Central Asian politics. Shahjahan fought a number of wars and for sometime was able to control Balkh and even seated his nominee on its throne.[69] The Mughals however had to retrace their steps. The Mughal chronicles do not speak of the reverses the Indian army faced. However, the Central Asian chronicles have a different story to tell. A large number of Indians were taken prisoners and sold into slavery in the markets of different towns such as Samarkand, Tashkent, etc., for five or six roubles each or even for less.[70] The Indian slaves in Balkh faced starvation and even firewood was not available in the winter months. To ward off cold, they warmed themselves first by burning the wooden handles of javelins, bows, arrows and palanquins and everything that could be burned. Eventually they even burnt the corpses of their compatriots to keep themselves warm.[71]

The fate of Indian slaves can be inferred from the experience of Aladinkhan, who reached Astrakhan in 1661. As a trader he had gone to Balkh fifteen years ago. After two years, having sold his goods, while returning home, he was enslaved and carried to Bukhara. There he lived for three years and was then sold to the Khivans. He was resold to a Tatar woman from where he escaped after stealing a horse. He was arrested at Cherno Yar where his horse was confiscated and was sent to Astrakhan. He then applied to the Tsar to allow him to become a Christian.[72]

Continual wars certainly impeded the flow of men and goods both ways. But once the wars had ceased, the visits of traders between the two areas continued subject only to local factors, such as famines, internal political instability, etc. Under Auragzeb, the exchange of embassies was resumed. The chronicler Saqui Musta 'ad Khan tells us about the exchange of envoys.[73]

Having ascertained that close contacts existed between India and Central Asia, the Russian ruler tried to gather information about trade routes to India via Central Asia through a variety of sources.[74] He was emboldened to do so after the envoy of Urgench, asked about the way to India and the possibilities of trade, had replied, "....traders between the two countries move freely and time involved in travel was two and half months. The goods brought by Indian traders were cotton textiles, etc., cloves, nutmegs, dyes..."[75].

The Russian Tsar sent a number of envoys and agents overland via Bukhara to the Mughal Empire in order to establish direct trade links.[76] In 1670 the Russian envoys B.A. Pazukhin and C.I. Pazukhin reported to the Tsar that the ruler of Balkh had informed them that the route between capital Balkh and Delhi ran through populous areas and life and property were absolutely safe and no extra-legal taxes were charged.[77]

When the Bukharan envoy was interviewed by Russian officers, he informed, "...at present merchants bring goods from India as they (belonging to both the countries) are continuously moving.... They bring precious stones and pearls and other items of luxury".[78]

One of these Russian envoys Muhammad Yusuf Kasimov reached Kabul in 1676 but was not allowed by Aurangzeb to come to Delhi and he returned home in 1677.[79]

Khoja Samandar Termezi the Author of *Dastur al-Muluk* written around 1695-96 describes Karshi or Nesef, as another emporium where goods from Kandahar and Central Asian cities such as Bukhara, Samarkand, Hissar, etc., were brought and exchanged by the respective traders.[80] At another place while writing about an administrator of Karshi he says that he covered the entire distance from Karshi to Jurgati with cloth from Gujarat taken from the local textile shops.[81] One cannot think that such plentitude of textiles from a region of India, thousands of miles away by land route could be brought only by Central Asian merchants. After all, a merchant carried horses from the port of Surat in Gujarat while Shahjahan was camping in Kabul. It is true, the two met somewhere between the rivers Jhelum and Chenab on 19 October 1646 since Shahjahan had left Kabul on 20 September 1646.[82] The price of horse was estimated at Rs. 15,000/- and it was named as 'Lal Bibaha' or priceless ruby.[83]

The Indians engaged in this trade generally came from Sindh, Rajasthan and the Punjab regions of our country and as I have earlier stated, they professed faith such as Hinduism, Sikhism and Islam, etc. However, some evidence of nineteenth century suggests that Indians from Mirzapur in Uttar Pradesh also travelled to Central Asia.

V

Indians, during the Mughal period, made significant contribution to Persian language and literature and were respected for their learning in Central Asia.

The decline of the Mughal empire after the death of Aurangzeb in 1707 did not put an end to visits of Indians to Central Asia.

The sources, now more abundant, such as *Russko-Indiiskiye Otnosheniya v XVIII V.*, Forster's *A Journey from Bengal to England,* Vol. II, Mohan Lal's *Travel in The Punjab, Afghanistan and Turkistan*, attest to the presence of Indians there in the eighteenth and nineteenth centuries.

But the Indians after performing these arduous journeys did not forget their homeland. They repeated to themselves, "जो सुख अपने चौबारे, ना बलख ना बुखारे "

"The pleasures that can be had in one's own courtyard cannot be had even in Balkh or Bukhara".

REFERENCES

1. Samuel Purchas, *Purchas His Pilgrimes*, Vol. IV, Glasgow, 1906, pp. 551, 552, 566.

2. Riazul Islam, *Indo-Persian Relations*, Teheran, 1970, p. 172.

3. A.A. Kunznetsov (ed.), *Khozhdeniye kuptsa Fedeta Kotova v Persiyu*, Moscow, 1958, p. 55. He describes them as worshippers of sun. He was in Persia in 1623.

4. Abul Fazl, *Ain-i-Akbari*, Delhi, 1989, Vol. II, p. 405.

5. *Ibid*, p. 406.

6. N.B. Novikova, *Rol Srednei Azii v Russko-Indiiskikh Torgovykh Svyazakh*, Tashkent, 1964, p. 25. For a detailed study of routes, please see H.C. Varma, *Medieval Routes to India,* Calcutta, 1978, Ch. II.

7. Purchas, IV, pp. 225-292.

8. Between 1368 and 1398 Timur sent nine embassies to China and the Chinese reciprocrated these gestures. O. Buriyev and A. Kolganov, "Ob Odnom Uchastke Velikogo Shelkogo Puti" in G.A. Pugachenkova (chief ed), *Na Sredne-aziatskikh trasakh velikogo shelkogo puti,* Tashkent, 1990, p. 108.

9. Ghiyasuddin Ali, *Dnevnik pokhoda Timura v Indiyu* (Russian version of 'Kitab Roznamai Ghazbat Hindustan Talif al Din Ali bin Jamal al-Salam'), Moscow, 1958, p. 125; Babur also recalls this in his autobiography. Babur, *Babur-Name* (Russian translation by S. Salye), Tashkent, 1958, p. 336.

10. *Babur-Name*, p. 167.

11. N.B. Baikova, *op. cit.*, pp. 11-12.

12. P.N. Rasul-zade, *Iz Istorii Sredne-Aziatsko-Indiiskikh Svyazei*, Tashkent, 1968, pp. 15-16.

13. O. Buriev and A. Kolganov, *loc.cit.,* p. 107.

14. A Urinboev, *Abdurrazzak Samarkandii ning Hindiston Safarnomasi* (in Uzbek), Tashkent, 1960, pp. 5 and 9.

15. N.A. Khalfin and P.M. Shastitko (eds.), *Rossiya i Indiya*, Moskva, 1976, p. 35.

16. Ya. G. Gulyamov (Chief Editor), *Istoriya Uzbekistan,* Tashkent, 1967, I, p. 537.

17. *Babur-Name*, p. 153.
18. *Ibid.*
19. *Ibid.*
20. *Istoriya Uzbekistan* I, p. 537.
21. Jauhar, *The Tezkerah Al Wakiat,* New Delhi, 1970, p. 118.
22. Yu. Sokolov, *Tashkent, Tashkentsy i Rossiya,* Tashkent, 1965, pp. 14-15.
23. Samuel Purchas, *Purchas His Pilgrimes,* Vol. XII, Glasgow, 1906, p. 24.
24. *Ibid,* p. 26.
25. R.G. Mukminova, *Sotsialnaya Differentsiatsia Naseleniya Gorodov Uzbekistana v XVI-XVI vv.* Tashkent, 1985, p. 120.
26. *Istoriya Uzbekistana,* I, p. 537.
27. *Babur-Name,* p. 153.
28. Bernier's *Travels in the Mogul Empire,* Trans. A. Constable, New Delhi, 1968, p. 203.
29. *Storia do Mogor*, II, trans. Irvine, London, 1907 pp. 390-91.
30. *Travels of Ibn Battuta*, p. 145 quoted in Iftikhar A. Khan, "Commerce In Horse Between Central Asia and India During Medieval Times," (Cyclostyled copy), p. 329.
31. Bernier, *op. cit.,* p. 249.
32. Jahangir, *The Tuzuk-i-Jahangiri*, Vol. I, Delhi, 1968, p. 350.
33. *Ibid.*
34. *Ibid.,* p. 422.
35. *Ibid.,* p. 428.
36. Bernier, *op. cit.,* p. 249.
37. *Ibid.,* p. 118.
38. Al Badaoni, *Muntakhabu-t-tawarikh*, Vol. II, Patna, 1973, pp. 278, 362, 365, 366.
39. *Indo-Persian Relations*, pp. 51, 53, 54.
40. R.G. Mukminova, *op. cit.,* p. 59.
41. *Ibid.,* pp. 60-61.
41. *Ibid.,* pp. 60-61.
43. *Ibid.,* pp. 60-61.

44. *Ibid.*, p. 61.
45. *Ibid.*, p. 62.
46. *Ibid.*, p. 63.
47. *Ibid.*, p. 65.
48. *Ibid.*, p. 66.
49. *Ibid.*, p. 112.
50. *Ibid.*, p. 113.
51. *Ibid.*, p. 114.
52. Bernier, *op. cit.*, p. 122.
53. Mukminova, *op. cit.*, p. 124.
54. *Ibid.*, pp. 122-23.
55. *Ibid.*, p. 123.
56. *Istoriya Uzbekistana*, p. 528.
57. Jahangir, *op. cit.,* p. 241.
58. *Ibid.*, p. 390.
59. *Ibid.*, II, *op. cit.,* p. 166.
60. Riazul Islam, *op.cit.,* p. 227.
61. Begley and Desai (eds.) *The Shah Jahan Name of Inayat Khan*, Delhi, 1990, pp. 270, 272, 281.
62. Jahangir, I, *op. cit.,* pp. 109-10.
63. *Purchas*, IV p. 269.
64. Niels Steensgaard, *The Asian Trade Revolution of the Seve p nteent Century,* Chicago, 1974, p. 410.
65. Goldberg, Antonva and Lavrentshova (eds.) *Russko-Indiiskiye Otnosheniya v XVII V.* (hereafter, *R-I.O. v XVII v.*) Moskva, 1958, Doc No. 13, p. 40.
66. Muhammad Yusuf Munshi, *Mukimkhanskaya Istoriya,* Tashkent, 1956, p. 84.
67. P.N. Rasul-zade, *op. cit.,* p. 17.
68. *Mukimkhanskaya Istoriya*, pp. 84-86.
69. *The Shah Jahan Nama of Inayat Khan*, pp. 343-51, 383-394, 446.
70. *Mukimkhankaya Istoriya,* p. 100.
71. *Ibid.*

72. *R-I.O. v XVII V.,* pp. 134-35.

73. Saqui Musta 'ad Khan, *Maasir-i-Alamgiri* (English translation by Jadunath Sarkar), pp. 41, 64, 87, 140, 203, 241; Nizamutdinov writes in detail about these embassies. An envoy of Aurangzeb Yakkataz Khan spent six years in Bukhara (1669-1675). I. Nizamutdinov., "Maasir-i-Alamgiri-Kak istochnik po vneshnopoliticheskim snosheniya Indii" in S.A. Azimzanova and I.M. Khasimov (eds.), *Indiya,* Tashkent, 1973, pp. 92-105.

74. *R-I.O. v XVII V.,* Doc. no. 85, p. 162.

75. *Ibid.,* p. 162; Nizamutdinov, loc. cit., p. 104. Aurangzeb sent his envoy to Khwarizm in 1670 and an envoy from Urgench (Khwarizm) arrived at his court in 1680.

76. *R-I.O. v XVII V.,* Doc. no. 91, pp. 168-70.

77. *Ibid.,* p. 170.

78. *Ibid.,* p. 171.

79. *Ibid.,* Doc. nos. 128, 132; pp. 222 and 224.

80. Khoja Samandar Termzi, *Dustur al-Muluk,* Moscow, 1971, p. 155.

81. *Ibid.,* p. 138.

82. *Shah Jahan Nama,* pp. 363, 365.

83. *Ibid.,* p. 365.

84. R.V. Ovchinnikov and M.A. Sidorov (Compilers), *Russko-Indiiskiye Otnosheniya v XVII V.,* Moskva, 1965; George Forster, *A Journey from Bengal to England,* Vol. II, Patiala, 1970; Mohan Lal, *Travel in The Punjab, Afghanistan and Turkistan.*

    To Bulkh, Bokhara And Herat And A Visit to Great Britain And Germany, Calcutta, 1977.

2

Indian Traders in Uzbekistan in the Eighteenth Century[*]

Surendra Gopal

I

Since the medieval times, records indicate the presence of Indian traders on the territory, today a part of the Republic of Uzbekistan.[1]

The population exchanges between India and Uzbekistan became more frequent after the Mughal rule was established in India in the first quarter of the sixteenth century. The Mughals hailed from that area and always retained fond memories of their homeland. Diplomats, scholars, artists, job-seekers, soldiers, mendicants, traders, etc., travelled between the two territories.

By the beginning of the eighteenth century, the four main exit points for Indians going to Uzbekistan extended from Kashmir in the north to Sind in the south. The launching point for a journey to Uzbekistan, at the northern most extremity, was from the valley of Kashmir to Leh to Yarkand and to Kashgar and then to the Farghana valley or on to Kokand. This route was mostly utilized by the Kashmiris.[1a]

The second exit point was Kabul, where traders, principally from the Punjab, generally known as Lahoris, assembled before

---

[*] *Historical and Cultural Links between India and Uzbekistan,* Patna, 1996, pp. 122-41.

going on to Balkh, Khulm or Tash Kargan, Kunduz, and other cities on the banks of the Oxus river. Thereafter they crossed over to the Uzbek territory. The term Lahoris generally denoted traders belonging to north-western and eastern Punjab. The Kashmiris also frequented this route. They travelled by the Srinagar, Muzaffarbad, Peshawar, Kabul road.

The third exit point of Indian traders was Multan. From Multan the merchants would generally march to Kandahar in Afghanistan. Here they would have the option either to go to the Persian territory directly or if they were interested in going to Central Asia, they could take the Kandahar-Ghazni-Kabul route and from Kabul go to the cities on the banks of the Oxus river and then enter the Uzbek area. These merchants could use several other routes to reach their destination in Uzbekistan. They could take the Kandahar-Ghazni-Herat route and from the last city they could go straight to Bukhara. They might also proceed from Herat to Mashad and then journey to Bukhara. All these roads were frequently used. Unsettled political conditions and temporary breakdown in the law and order only adversely affected the intensity of trade in the area, but did not disrupt it altogether.

Indian merchants using Multan as the point of departure were known as 'Multanis'. They however hailed from a much wider area which roughly covered western and lower Punjab (including Bahawalpur) and also the Rajasthan region.

A widely-used caravan route connected Multan with Bikaner in Rajasthan. We reach this conclusion as we come across a number of names of Indian merchants resident in Iran and Astrakhan in the eighteenth century with the surname Marwari *i.e.* one belonging to Marwar, the popular name of Rajasthan in those days.[1b]

Another group of Indian merchants known as 'Shikarpuris' were also to be found on the Uzbek territory. They derived their name from Shikarpur, a small town in Sukkur district in upper Sindh. The term Shikarpuris virtually covered merchants belonging to the whole of Sindh. They either went to Multan and used any of the options available to the Multanis or sometimes, they went straight to Kandahar from where they took the road either to Persia or to the Uzbek country using either Kabul or Herat or Mashad as their final launching point.[2]

At this juncture some more facts about Indians going to Central Asia including Uzbekistan should be noted.

First, the Lohanis an Afghan tribe residing on the borders of Afghanistan, Baluchistan and the Punjab played a significant role in this trade, both as traders as well as carriers of commodities, especially those emanating from Multan.

The Muslim component among the Indian traders is hard to identify as they easily mingled with the overwhelmingly Muslim population of the area and became indistinguishable from them in terms of dress, religion and many of their social and religious rituals. It is this factor which induces a lower estimate of the number of Indian traders moving out of the country by the land-route for Iran, Afghanistan, Central Asia and for lands beyond the above-mentioned territories.

Also it must be noted that these exit points were never the monopoly of any exclusive group. The Kashmiris could come down to Kabul either by crossing the Punjab or Badakhshan and then cross over to the Uzbek territory. The merchants from Kabul going to Badakhshan could travel to Yarkand and Kashgar and enter the Farghana valley. The 'Lahori merchants' could sail down the river Ravi, reach Multan and then decide on the road they would take for reaching the trans-Oxus region, either by traversing Afghanistan or both Afghanistan and north-east Iran.

It may also be noted that traders from other parts of India also mingled with those from Kashmir, Lahore, Multan and Shikarpur and visited Central Asia.

Finally, Indians residing in different parts of Iran and Astrakhan also took advantage of the business opportunities available in Central Asia.

The Indians going to the Uzbek territory from their base of operations in Iranian cities belonged especially to Yezd. But the Indian merchants well-established in several cities of Iran, situated near the Persian Gulf or in the lands bordering on the west and south of the Caspian Sea or in Khorasan, *i.e.* north-eastern Iran[4] also occasionally travelled to Bukhara. Many of these cities had continuous trade links with Bukhara and other places in Uzbekistan and the Indians residing there were well aware of the route, the commodities and the general commercial environment in Central Asia.

Finally, the Indians, who had lived in the Russian port-town of Astrakhan since the seventeenth century also carried on trade with the Uzbek country after crossing the Khivan territory. This was the outcome of the relationship that had developed between the Indian and Bukharan traders staying in Astrakhan. We come across several instances of contacts between Indians and Bukharan merchants residing in the Bukhara shopping arcade in Astrakhan.

It can thus be seen, that in the eighteenth century the Indians flocked to Uzbekistan and Central Asia from a large number of places in India, Afghanistan, Iran and Russia.

II

The Indians going to Uzbekistan and Central Asia not only came from different parts of India but they also professed a variety of faiths.

The names of these merchants show that they were Hindus, Jains, Sikhs and Muslims.

The number of emigrant Indian Muslim traders cannot be ascertained as they became indistinguishable from the local population or they became a part of the Iranian or Afghan mercantile groups because of similarity of religious beliefs and largely identical life-styles.

The non-Muslim Indians practised their own religions, and as far as possible, retained many of their social practices and features of their traditional life-style. They smeared their foreheads with sandal paste, brought priests from their homeland to assist them in following their religion, and above all, they continued to cremate the bodies of their deceased co-religionists.[5]

In the Uzbek territory their distinct identity was recognised; in Bukhara they lived in a special serai even in the seventeenth century as revealed by a distinguished contemporary historian.

It should be interesting to explore the factors which enabled groups of non-Muslim merchants to establish themselves on the Uzbek territory. Their journey to Uzbekistan and Central Asia across inhospitable mountainous and desert terrain in Afghanistan and Iran was greatly facilitated by the presence of Hindu traders in all the important trade centres and halting places in both the countries. A continuous chain of Indian traders on the roads leading from the borders of India to Central Asia existed. This kept an Indian's line of contact back home intact. He was also provided with business intelligence, and given support in terms of food, shelter, merchandise, etc. Of course, the number of Indians varied according to the size and the importance of each business centre. A quick look at resident Indians in the different business centres of Afghanistan and Iran illustrates this point.

III

Let us take the example of Kandahar, the starting point for the journeys undertaken by the Shikarpuris and Multanis. Forster who visited the place in the late 1790s noted, "At Kandahar are established many Hindu families chiefly of Multan and many Rajput districts, who by their industry and mercantile knowledge, have essentially augmented its wealth and trade.... The extensive range of shops occupied by Hindu traders with the ease and contentment expressed in their deportment affords a fair testimony of their enjoying at Kandahar, liberty and protection".[6] Elphinstone in the first decade of the nineteenth century wrote about the Hindu merchants of Kandahar, "The Hindus have the best houses of the common people, and adhere to their custom of building them very high".[7]

India and Central Asia

Elphinstone while reporting Mr. Christie's visit at the opening of the nineteenth century stated that the latter went to a Shikarpuri street there.[8] This underlines the strong presence of the Hindu traders in Kandahar, the trade emporium of India, Iran, Afghanistan and Central Asia.

As regards Kabul, Forster admitted, "Among the foreign nations who frequent the city, the Hindus, chiefly of Peshour contribute more than any other to enrich it, by superior industry and knowledge of commerce;.... the Hindus of Kabul are indebted, for special indulgence to the one of their sect who controls the revenues of the Shah, and stands high in favour."[9] In Balkh or Bala Hissar, which marked the last outpost on the soil of Afghanistan before the Indians crossed the Oxus river and set their foot on the Central Asian soil, the Hindu traders were present in substantial numbers. The Indians who reached Balkh on way to Central Asia were not obstructed by the Afghan authorities.[10]

The presence of Hindu merchants was marked in Herat—an important road junction between Afghanistan, Iran and Central Asia. It had an exclusive caravan-serai for the Indian merchants. Pottinger estimated the number of Hindu merchants at Herat to be at 600.[11] They were described as 'only persons who possess capital'.[12] They lived in the best serais which had gardens outside.[13] Pottinger on way from Herat to Mashad found Hindu shopkeepers in small villages and isolated serais.[14] At Herat he was provided with a guide by his Hindu agent.[15]

It was said, "Herat owes its prosperity to the great commerce it enjoys, being the only channel of communication between the east and west of Asia, all the trade and produce of Cabul, Cashmere and India from one side and of Bukhara, Persia, Arabia, Turkey and even Europe on the other, must pass through this city...,"[16].

The presence of the Hindus all over Afghanistan was commented upon by Elphinstone. He noted, "...The Hindus...are to be found over the whole Kingdom of Cabul... In towns they are in considerable numbers as brokers, merchants, bankers, goldsmiths, seller of grains, etc. There is scarce a village in the country without a family or two who exercise the above trades and act as accountants, money-changers e&c. They spread into the north of Persia, but in small numbers, owing to the bad treatment they receive. They are encouraged in Bokhara and other towns of Tartary."[17]

The Shikarpuris were also fairly wide-spread in the region. "Shikarpuri bankers are to be found in every part of the Dooranee dominions, and in all towns of Toorkistan."[18]

Fraser found Indians of Bohra sect at Yezd in 1820.[19] The city was situated at the meeting of roads between Iran, Afghanistan and Central Asia. He further stated that at Yezd, "all the merchandise of India, Cabul, Cashmere, Bukhara, etc. and are met there by merchants from Ispahan, Sheeraz, Cashan, Teheran, and other parts of Persia."[20]

Mashad, in Iran with its mausoleum of Imam Ali, also had a sizeable number of Indians both merchants as well as pilgrims. Fraser met a Kashmiri mendicant at Nishan Ablee.[21] When he looked for Hindu merchants he found only two from Kandahar. He commented that this was not formerly the case; 'at one time Mashad[22] was the resort of many affluent Hindoos, but oppression and distracted state of country had driven wealth of all its successful votaries far away from Persia'.[23] They, however, met many merchants from Bukhara here.

Merv, another important town, which lay at the crossroads between Iran, the Turkoman territory Bukhara and Afghanistan and which was almost equidistant from Bhokhara[24], Mashad, Khiva, Balkh and Herat also had a colony of Indian merchants.[25] The people were found to be dressed either in Persian or Indian textiles and the Indian merchants regularly visited it.[26] The Indians sold here indigo, valuable brocade, white and fine muslin. They carried Russian goods to India.[27]

IV

The Indians were able to gain access to important trade centres in Central Asia because of the presence of their compatriots in all towns in north-east Iran and Afghanistan, which had active links with Central Asia. The above mentioned circumstances also enabled the Indian traders, stationed in Astrakhan on the Caspian Sea since the seventeenth century, to trade with Bukhara because the Russian port-town had regular commercial contacts with Bukhara via the Khivan territory.[28] Also Astrakhan's trade links with Iranian cities located on the southern and eastern edge of the Caspian Sea facilitated the trade of Indians with Central Asia, since these Iranian cities had been already exchanging goods with Central Asia. In 1721 a caravan from Astrakhan to Bukhara via Khiva carried more Indian than Russian goods.[29]

There is ample evidence to show that cordial relations that existed between the Indian traders and Bukharans in Astrakhan, helped Indians to keep up trade with Bukhara. A Bukharan resident of the Bukharan caravan-serai borrowed money from an Indian trader.[30] In another instance, a Bukharan trader took loan from an Indian to go to Bukhara.[31] A Multani lived in Bukharan caravan-serai.[32] In 1726 Indians from Astrakhan prayed for passage through Khiva to Bukhara.[33] In 1732, Indians from Astrakhan sent goods to Khiva and Bukhara.[34] Many Bukharans living in Astrakhan used to act as agents of the Indian merchants.[35]

In sum, it can be asserted that the wide dispersal of non-Muslim and Muslim Indian traders in both Afghanistan and Iran and their concentration in Astrakhan enabled them to extend their operations to the cities of Uzbekistan and Central Asia. Bukhara had emerged as the chief point of concentration of the Indians. Pospelov, a Russian engineer who was sent by the Tsar to Tashkent in 1800 noted that Bukhara supplied Russian, Chinese, Persian and Indian commodities. He further commented "From Bukhara it is possible to secure Indian and Persian commodities which are available there in large quantities and this trade may be expanded further with the assistance of Persia."[35a]

V

One would like to examine the reasons for this diffusion of the Indian mercantile community in the principal cities of Afghanistan and north-east Iran.

First, the uninterrupted Mughal rule in the sixteeth and the seventeenth centuries over large parts of Afghanistan helped to integrate its economy with that of the Indian subcontinent. Also the Mughals sent Hindu governors, administrative functionaries and contingents of Rajput soldiers to uphold the Mughal rule and administer the area on their behalf. Such a favourable political and administrative situation helped non-Muslim Indian mercantile groups to establish themselves in Afghanistan.[36]

The Indo-Iranian trade exchanges had a long history and were based on the supply of mutually needed goods. Hence Indians, both Muslims and non-Muslims were going to Iran both by the land as well as the sea routes.

The Mughal rule positively strengthened the trade ties between the two countries. Its contribution was especially valuable in the field of overland trade. The Safavid and the Mughals had a common international frontier; their relations were generally cordial; regular exchange of embassies took place between both the countries even when relations had temporarily soured; the Mughals welcomed Iranian soldiers, administrators, etc., and extended patronage to them.[37] Consequently the common Indian going to Iran generally did not meet with a hostile reception. This helped Indians, both Muslims and non-Muslims, to emerge as a significant merchant group in the seventeenth century.[37a]

But the most important reason which enabled the Indian and chiefly the non-Muslim Indian mercantile group to thrive was the nature of economic services rendered by them to the local economy and the local populace.

The Indians, who were spread all over Iran, Afghanistan, Uzbekistan, other parts of Central Asia and India, were a great help in the transmission of money through letters of credit. This was a very useful economic function, especially in a situation where as Fraser noted, "...Bills of exchange are neither common, nor much understood..."[38] Of course, the Indians earned great profit out of it. Fraser found, "...but when any merchant gives an order upon his agent at a distant place, for instance, on Shikarpore or takes a Bill to accommodate another; he exacts a very high rate of exchange, often from twenty to twenty-five per cent."[39] Pottinger carried a Bill for two hundred rupees which was discounted by a Hindu trader, who also accompanied him to local places and gave him necessary guidance.[40]

From 1720s the hold of the Mughals began to slacken in Afghanistan as they had entered a period of decline. The Afghans, supplanted the Safavids and managed to dominate Iran. They politically unified Iran and Afghanistan, a circumstance which enabled the traders to continue their activity over this area. Political change did not hamper trade, except temporarily.

Soon Nadir Shah, an Iranian drove out the Afghans from Iran. He eventually annexed Afghanistan and in 1730s and 1740s extended his conquest to Delhi, the Trans-Oxiana and Azerbaijan.[41] Under Nadir Shah even a bigger politically unified region had been created which included all the places where Indian merchants had been active in Afghanistan, Iran, the Caucasus region and Central Asia.

Nadir Shah after his victiories in India, sent Indian artisans such as masons, [41a] stone-cutters, carpenters, etc., to construct grandiose buildings in Balkh and Central Asian cities. By importing Indian artists and artisans, he was merely repeating what other Central Asian rulers had done in the seventeenth century.

The recurrent wars, march of soldiers, collapse of local administration, etc., caused only temporary dislocation in trade in the first half of the eighteenth century, and did not significantly affect or alter the pattern of customary trade.

After Nadir Shah's assassination in 1747, almost an identical role was played by the Afghan warrior Ahmed Shah Abdalee, who once again brought the whole of Afghanistan under his control, extended his hold over part of Trans-Oxiana, Iran and up to Delhi in India.

In short, even major wars in the first half of the eighteenth century did not disrupt the political unity of the region. They appeared to have actually reinforced it and by forging a centralised control, created a favourable situation for the development of trade in the region, roughly extending from the Caspian Sea to the Yamuna river. Abdalees managed to keep their power intact over a large part of North-Western India, Afghanistan, North-Eastern Iran and parts of Central Asia virtually till the end of the eighteenth century and thereby ensured the continuity of the traditional pattern of commerce.

Ahmed Shah Abdalee ruled till 1773 and after his death his son Timur Shah managed to hold on to the Punjab till 1793. It was only after his death that under Zaman Shah the Afghan rule was replaced by that of the Sikhs over the Punjab and part of Afghanistan.[42] The reign of Timur Shah was long remembered as a time when Kabul "enjoyed its greatest modern prosperity. Timur Shah was a liberal-minded ruler, and was known to lend a man money, and tell them to go and trade with it."[43]

In the Abdalee empire the Indian traders were called upon to play an important role in the management of financial affairs. They transmitted the surplus of the local taxes left after meeting administrative expenses to the Central authority. They were also employed to look after the finances of nobility and the royalty.[44]

Elphinstone commented, "...the duty of treasurer or steward about every great man is exercised either by a Hindu or a Persian."[45] Consequently the Hindus in Afghanistan were fairly prosperous, "...many often they are in good circumstances and that they possess the best houses in every town, if we except the palace of the nobility."[46]

Elphinstone further found out that most of the business of banking was into the hands of Hindus. "They derive their profits from lending money, which they do at an enormous interest, by negotiating bills of exchange, and by transactions connected with the fluctuations of the exchange in the place where they reside. Another source of profit arises from advancing money to government for bill on the revenue of the provinces, and this hazardous speculation is recommended by a premium, always large and increasing with the rush of non-payment. Some of the bankers are very rich...."[47]

"...the bankers much desire such security from the great Doorrounees putting money into their hands to be employed to the best advantage, a practice which indentifies the interests of the bankers and the nobility. Needy nobles also afford their protection to bankers, and treat them with great attention, in the hope of being able to borrow money from them; and like other classes of industrious people, they derive benefit from the obvious interest which King has in protecting them against individuals of his own nation."[48]

Elphinstone has thus shown that the Hindu merchants performed many useful functions; they were the moneylenders; they lent money not only to individuals but also to the government; they guaranteed to the government the transmission of taxes collected all over the kingdom; their extensive net-work all over Afghanistan ensured this.

The presence of prosperous Hindu merchants throughout Afghanistan enabled the Hindu merchants to cross over to the adjoining region of Iran, Trans-Oxiana and beyond for trade since the lines of communication back home remained intact and in case of need, they could expect the support of their compatriots.

VI

As a result of such favourable circumstances the Indian merchants were found in Bukhara in fair numbers. In 1736 it was reported that three hundred Indians had left for Kabul after attacks by marauders.[49] Almost a century later Vigne reported that there were about two hundred houses of Hindus at Bukhara.[50] Several Hindus had left the city after the Ameer of Bukhara had disallowed cremation of the dead bodies of their co-religionists.[51]

In Bukhara the Hindu merchants lived in the Serai Tahakue. They paid one *Tila* (a gold coin) per month for one room. They sent poll tax (*Jiziya*) to the king. They mostly traded in indigo.[52]

Kashmiri merchants had established their houses in Bukhara, Samarkand, Kashgar, Yarkand, Khotan, Kathmandu, Bhutan, etc.[52a]

Among the imports by Indians in Bukhara, indigo constituted the chief commodity. Both Multan and Kabul were the principal points for the export of this dye. An early nineteenth century estimate puts the value of annual export of indigo from Multan at 40 to 50 thousand poods,[53] costing between 25 and 30 roubles per pood.*

The next important commodity imported by them was sugar of different varieties.

Besides, white muslin from India was always in great demand especially for use as head-gear and turban. White calicoes of Punjab[54] were also sent to the region. *Lungis* were also supplied. The Multani cotton-textiles were also favoured by local consumers, especially the chintzes.[55]

Vigne in 1830s noted 'a special Cafila of camels' burdened with indigo purchased at Multan and Bahawalpur and chintz of Hindustan. Some part of this investment finds its way to Bukhara...'[56]

Among miscellaneous items exported to Bukhara were shoes with upper of cloth, embroidered with gold.[57]

Several varieties of silken textiles manufactured at Multan were also extremely popular. The ulemas at Mawran-ul-Nahar were found dressed in clothes brought from Banaras and known as *'nehree Khab'* and *'sade-abreshim'*.[57a]

The importance of Multan as a weaving centre of silken textiles is not surprising in view of the fact that in the mid-eighteenth century Multan imported silk from Bengal, Kashmir, China, Bukhara and Turkistan.[57b]

A Dutch account of mid 1770s states that 1649 maunds of silk were exported to Multan from Bengal. 'It was the third highest quantity after Mirzapur and Lahore. Lahore imported 3,851 maunds of silk'.[57c] The Lohani merchants brought 'seven hundred maunds of raw silk to Multan every year from Bukhara and Turkistan'.[57d]

The imported raw silk was woven into textiles in one hundred and fifty workshops.[57e]

---

*Pood or Pud is a Russian measure of weight equivalent to 16 kgs.

A very popular item in demand in Uzbekistan was Kashmiri shawl, which was prized not only as an item of status symbol but also as a form of valuable personal property.[58]

A Kashmiri shawl was placed over the body of the Naqshabandi Khwaja when he was being laid to rest after his death.[59]

The Kashmiri shawls and other woolen garments were prized possessions even beyond the confines of Uzbekistan. The Russian authorities sent Mekhti Rafailov and others to explore the markets of eastern Turkistan and Kashmir.[60] The popularity of Kashmiri shawls had increased when during the first half of the eighteenth century, new techniques were developed and embroidery improved.[60a]

Several other items produced in Kashmir were exported to Bukhara and the Central Asia region. These included saffron, edible oil, honey and red chillies via the Gilgit route. Ornamented shoes from Kashmir were also exported to Central Asia. Another Kashmiri item highly prized in Central Asian markets was jade utensils, made by Kashmiri artisans from jade brought from Yarkand.

This route was almost exclusively monopolised by Kashmiri merchants, who constituted a well-identified group among Indian traders in Central Asia. Since Kashmiri commodities were readily saleable, the Kashmiris were to be found in almost all the prominent cities of Central Asia.

An idea of the total volume of export to Bukhara may be had from the following statement of Vigne, "Beside the Lohanis there are five or six *kafilas* which annually pass the Hindoo Koosh for Bokhara, laden with various wares."[61]

Indians also carried pearls, diamonds and gems to Bukhara.[61a] These were held high in popular esteem. As a result when the Russians established the city of Orenburg to carry on trade with Bukhara and India,[62] many Bukharan merchants carried Indian goods, especially diamonds and gems for selling them there.[63] Some of these diamonds and gems were sent to England for being worked upon.[64]

The trade of Bukharans in Indian precious stones was so flourishing and profitable that the Russian merchants tried to confine their activities to Orenburg and prevented the access of Bukharans to Moscow by various means.[65]

VII

The popularity of Indian goods in Orenburg, emboldened, once in a while, some Indians to carry precious stones and printed textiles from the Deccan to Orenburg.[66]

The flourishing trade in Indian commodities in Orenburg, meant very good business for some Bukharan traders. We have the example of the Bukharan trader Irnazar Maksyutov who from 1745 onwards, for almost three decades, carried Indian goods not only to Orenburg but also to other towns of the Kazakh steppes. The Russian government commended his services and the officers of the Tsar in Orenburg repeatedly rewarded him for bringing in 'Indian brocade, valuable stones and other goods' and also for inducing not only Bukharans but also Indians for trading in Orenburg.[67]

The importance of Orenburg as a market for Indian goods became so high that when anarchy overtook Iran immediately after the death of Nadir Shah, Indian goods and coins were brought there and were presented for sale.[68]

The participation in the Orenburg trade even on a limited scale due to restrictions imposed by the Bukharan and Russian ruling circles, was a symbol of the dynamism of Indian traders. With their base in Bukhara, they had tried to extend the area of their operations when the opportunity presented itself. Without state support, they ventured to travel over long distances overland in an unknown and maybe even in an hostile territory risking both their lives and capital. One has to bow to their entrepreneurial abilities.[69]

While participating in the Orenburg trade, the Indians carried on their business activities in Bukhara. They lived in an exclusive caravan-serai, as the Khivans, the Kokandis, the Afghans and the Russians did. They sold their goods in wholesale principally to the Bukharan merchants.[70]

The value and volume of trade in Indian goods in Orenburg was so high that the Russian authorities thought of opening direct trade between Orenburg and India via Bukhara and for organising this trade, they invited an Indian trader, Marwari Barayev from Astrakhan.

Marwari Barayev reached Ufa on 26 February 1735 and stayed there for almost a year.[71] The effort did not succeed.

But the dream of establishing direct trade contacts with Indians did not fade.

Two Tatars, Nadir Saferov and Yagoferov in 1753 were sent to India with goods. Again Tatar merchants were sent to India from Orenburg.[72]

Another merchant from Orenburg, Gaibaiddulah Amirov spent thirty years between 1775 and 1805 in India. He travelled around eleven thousand kilometres and visited even the eastern metropolis of Calcutta.[73] He recommended to the Russian authorities the Bukhara-Kabul-Delhi-Calcutta route which according to his calculations required a journey of 219 days.[74]

VII

In course of the eighteenth century, the repeated efforts of Tsarist officials to develop Orenburg as a transit point for direct trade with India failed. The Russian authorities in the beginning of the nineteenth century began to promote another city Semiplatinsk established in 1718 as an exit point for their trading caravans going to eastern Turkistan and northern India.[75] From 1804 foreign traders began bringing in Kashmiri shawls which fetched in Russia the fantastic price between one thousand roubles and fifteen thousand roubles per piece.[76] Hence, in August 1808 these traders led by Mekhti Rafailov left for eastern Turkistan and they returned in March 1811 after visiting Kulja, Aksu, Kashgar, Yarkand and Kashmir.[77]

Sporadic attempts were made by Indians in Bukhara to trade with Siberia as well. In 1764 they visited Siberia with their goods.[78]

Other places in Uzbekistan also attracted Indian traders. Speaking of Mawra-al-Nahar, Fraser reported, "A regular intercourse is kept up with. . . Herat, Cabul, Peshawar, Shikarpur, Budakhshan, Kashmir, Kitai and all the countries dependent thereupon."

"From Cabul, Peshawar, Shikarpur and these quarters they receive wool, turbans, white cotton cloth, chintz, sugar in all shapes, yellow stock for dyes, spices, black papper, law books. In return they send horses, copper,. . .gilt copper wire, turquoises, coral silk, tea and China stuff."[79]

The emergence of Shikarpuri Hindus as an important mercantile group among Indians towards the closing decades the eighteenth century was an important event. These hailed from Shikarpur in the Sukkar district in upper Sindh. They appeared to have gained in importance after Timur Shah, the ruler of Afghanistan granted them full religious protection in 1785.[79a] Soon they were to be found not only in Afghanistan but also in major cities of Iran and Trans-Oxiana. In Central Asia, their major concentration was in Bukhara though many were also to be found in places such as Tashkent, Kokand, etc. They thrived throughout the nineteenth century and were known more for their moneylending and banking operations than trade.

At Kunduz, the Uzbeks were respectful to the Indians and treated them as elder brothers.[80]

Besides trade, the Hindu merchants in Bukhara and other Uzbek towns had also emerged as moneylenders as in Astrakhan. They supplied small as well as big credit. In fact, they were identified more as 'moneylenders' than as traders.[81]

Obviously, the decision of the Bukhara authorities to confine Indians to whole-sale trade was meant to restrict their activities. This was one reason why they, as a group, could never realise the full potential of their entrepreneurial abilities as the European trading companies in India did in the eighteenth century.

The Indians were forced to stick to trade only in those items in which they were allowed by the local authorities. They took to moneylending, which was taboo to Muslims according to Islamic orthodoxy. As the next century proceeded, this was the main activity on which they concentrated. They had now no incentive to expand their trading operations. Economically they stagnated. Also, as moneylenders they became an object of derision in the local society; they lost status and went down in popular esteem.

Occasionally, Indian artisans, especially goldsmiths could also be found in the Uzbek territory. Elphinstone met a Sikh goldsmith who had travelled over great parts of Afghanistan, Persia, Khorasan and Tartary.[82]

From later accounts we know that Kashmiri artisans, especially those who knew the art of mending costly silk, and woollen garments were frequent visitors to the cities of Uzbekistan.

Among the goods exported from Uzbekistan, horses occupied the most important place. Of course, horses from Baluchistan and Khorasan were also regularly brought to India.[83] But Uzbek horses commanded the best prices.

The Uzbek merchants brought horses to Herat where they were sold from rupees one thousand to four thousand each.[84]

Horses bred around Balkh were sent to Kabul and then to India.[85]

Kashmir also regularly imported war horses from Central Asia.[85a]

Other goods brought from Bukhara included copper, Ilanche cloth, saddle of horses, turquoise, raw silk and embroidered cloth.[86]

Other imports from Bukhara into India consisted of pomegranates, almonds, ruwash from Kabul; and from Bukhara horse, cochineal, nankin, gold thread, raw silk and other goods.[87]

Rugs and carpets from Turkistan were brought to Multan. Their designs were later on copied by the local workers and exported to other parts of India where they were prized for their durability and fineness.[87a]

Let it not be said that only Indian merchants visited Uzbekistan.

In the eighteenth century, the merchants of Tashkent, situated on the northeast corner of Uzbekistan, visited Russian cities in Siberia such as Petropavlovsk, Semiplatinsk, Troitsk, Orsk, Orenburg, etc., with their merchandise, in groups as well as individually[87b]. The journey involved crossing the steppes, and use often accompanied by armed guards. These traders also visited Kashgar and commercial centres in India and Afghanistan.[88]

In fact, merchants from Azerbaijan, northeast Iran and Uzbekistan were also in the habit of frequenting India with their goods. Kazim while accompanying the army of Nadir Shah met two traders from Derbent who had travelled to Iraq, Khorasan, to Kandahar, Kabul, Jalalabad, Peshawar and Multan. He found them on way to Lahore.[89]

Many Bukharans in Herat expressed a desire to go to Kandahar.[90]

However it is difficult to state with precision the number of Central Asian merchants coming to India. True, in the eighteenth century, the Mughal power was inexorably moving towards its demise; the Central Asian merchants lost a powerful incentive—the court patronage. The royalty and the nobility were no longer their best customers.

IX

As the century ended, new forces destined to greatly influence relations between India and Central Asia appeared.

Throughout the eighteenth century the Russians had desperately tried to establish regular trade with India via the overland route. Experience had shown that this would remain a dream unless they had a firm base in Central Asia, especially in the Trans-Oxiana region. Hence, from the beginning of the nineteenth century, military expeditions to annex Central Asian territory began to figure in their calculations.

In the meanwhile, the British firmly entrenched in India, were worrying about the Russian advance in Central Asia as they felt that the Russians would eventually threaten their position and possessions in India. This colonial rivalry started what came to be known as 'The Great Game'.[91]

The two powers viewed with great suspicion each other's efforts to secure influence and dominance in Central Asia by all available means. 'The Great Game' continued throughout the nineteenth century in which the Indians and Central Asians were used as pawns. It affected the pattern of Indian trade and the exodus of Indian merchants to Central Asia in the nineteenth century.[92]

REFERENCES

1. Surendra Gopal, "Indians in Central Asia 16th and 17th Centuries," *Proceedings,* Indian History Congress, 52nd Session, Delhi, 1992, pp. 219-31

1a. A number of variations of this route was possible. For details of various routes. See A.M. Mattoo, "Commercial Interaction Between Kashmir & Central Asia", *The Journal of Central Asian Studies*, Srinagar, Vol. 3, No. 1, 1992, pp. 36-39.

   Kashmiris could go from Yarkand to Badakhshan, Idem, p. 37, Trade routes from Kashmir, Beijing, Samarkand and Bukhara converged on the territory of Kashgar, Idem, p. 38. See also P.N. Rasul-Zade, *Is istorii sredne-azaiatsko-indiiskih svyazei vtoroi poloviny XIX-nachala XX veka*, Tashkent, 1968, p. 21.

   The commercial ties of Tashkent with Kashgar were so intimate that the city had a quarter named Kashgar. Yu. Sokolov, *Tashkent, Tashkenttsi i Rossiya*, Tashkent, 1965, p. 27.

1b. B.L. Gupta, "The migration of Traders to Rajasthan in the eighteenth century, *Proceedings,* IHC, 48th session, Goa, 1988, pp. 312-17.

2. I.H. Siddiqui (tr.) *Tarikh-i-Manazil-i-Bukhara*, Srinagar, 1982, p. 35. No Hindu owned a house in Bukhara.

3. G.T. Vigne, *A Personal Narrative of a Visit to Ghuzni, Kabul, Afghanistan*, First published 1840, Delhi, 1986 pp. 44, 54, 56, 57. They were treated well by the rulers of the Punjab and Afghanistan. They carried goods even from Jaipur in Rajasthan and Calcutta in Bengal.

4. See my paper, "Indian Traders in Persia in the Seventeenth Century" *Journal of Historical Studies*, Patna, No. 2, Dec. 1996, pp. 14-36.

5. *Mukimkhanskaya Istoriya*, p. 84; Surendra Gopal, *loc. cit.*, pp. 219-31.

6. George Forster, *A Journey from Bengal to England*, Language Department, Punjab, 1970, Vol. II, p. 115. Forster had travelled from Srinagar to Kabul via the Punjab and then to Kandhar.

7. Mountstuart Elphinstone, *An Account of the Kingdom of Cabul*, Vol. II, OUP, Karachi, p. 113.

8. *Ibid.*, p. 362.

9. Forster, II, p. 83.

10. Elphinstone II, p. 183.

11. Pottinger, p. 415.

12. *Ibid.*

13. *Ibid.*

14. *Ibid.*, pp. 417, 419, 420.

15. *Ibid,* 417.

16. Fraser, pp. 31-32.

17. Elphinstone I, p. 414.

18. Elphinstone II, p. 231.

19. Fraser, *Narrative of a Journey to Khorasan in the Years 1821 & 1822*, Delhi, 1984, p. 375.

20. *Ibid.*, p. 22.

21. *Ibid.*, p. 493; An Indian Nawab had passed through Mashad on way to Kerbela, *Ibid.*, p. 335.

22. *Ibid.*, 481; The Indian Shia Muslims regarded these centres as places of pilgrimage and visited them.

23. *Ibid.*, p. 482.

24. Vigne, *A Personal Narrative of a Visit to Ghuzni, Kabul and Afghanistan*, p. 55.

25. Fraser, p. 55.

26. K.A. Antonova and N.M. Goldberg (eds.), *Russko-Indiskiya Otnosheniya v XVIII v* (hereafter cited as *R-I. O. v XVIII v.*, pp. 564-65.

27. *Ibid,* p. 565

28. *Ibid.*, p. 521

29. *Ibid.*, p. 57, no. 36

30. *Ibid.*, pp. 64, 96, 210

31. *Ibid.*, p. 65

32. *Ibid.*, p. 71

33. *Ibid.,* pp. 72, 73, 20, 46
34. *Ibid.,* p. 116
35. *Ibid.,* no. 191
35a. cited in Rasul-zade, p. 20
36. A historian who accompanied Nadir Shah on his campaign to India reported that 12,000 Rajputs resided in the fort of Kabul. Muhammad Kazim, *Pokhod Nadir Shaha v Indiyu,* Moskva, 1961, p. 42.
37. Sadat Khan Nishapuri came to Delhi, was appointed to an important position by the Mughal ruler, eventually became the Nawab of Oudh. Ibid., pp. 102-3.
37a. Surendra Gopal, "Aspects of Indo-Persian trade in the seventeenth century," *Proceedings,* Indian History Congress, Varanasi, 1969, pp. 240-6.
38. Fraser, p. 95.
39. *Ibid.*
40. Pottinger, p. 406-407.
41. Muhammad Kazim, pp. 7-8. Kandahar was captured by the Afghans in 1709 and Nadir Shah besieged for two years between 1736 and 1738 before finally conquering it and marching on to India.
41a. Sir William Jones, *History of Nadirshah,* Vol. I, Delhi, n.d., p. 462.
42. *Armeniya pod vlastyu Ahmad Shah Durani* p. XIII; Gankovsky, *Imperiya Durrani,* Moskva, 1958, p. 24. Shikarpur in Sindh remained under the control of the Afghans till 1824.
43. Vigne, p. 376
44. Elphinstone, I, p. 414
45. *Ibid.*
46. *Ibid.,* p. 415
47. *Ibid.,* p. 333
48. *Ibid.,* p. 335
49. *R-I.O. v XVII* v., p. 139
50. Vigne, p. 165
51. *Ibid.*
52. *Tarikh-i-Manazil-i-Bukhara,* p. 50
52a. A.M. Mattoo, *loc. cit.,* p. 39
53. Shastitko, *Rossiskiye Puteshestvenniki v Indii XIX-nachalo XX v.,* Moskva, 1990, p. 52.

54. *Tarikh-i-Manazil-i-Bukhara*, p. 34.

55. The demand for cotton textiles from the Punjab was very great in Afghanistan. Vigne noted that every writer in a Cafila of three or four hundred camels was sent into the plains of Dera Bund and Dera Ameel Khan laden with madder roots. Out of its proceeds, they purchased a sufficient quantity of coarse clothes of the Punjab as supply for the whole of their tribe. Vigne, p. 107.

56. Vigne, p. 67

57. *Tarikh-i-Manazil-i-Bukhara*, p. 34

57a. Fraser, p. 83

57b. Dr. Humaira Dasti, "Multan As A Centre of Trade and Commerce During The Mughal Period", *Journal of the Pakistan Historical Society*, Vol. XXXVIII, July 1990, Part III, p. 251.

57c. Sushil Chaudhury, "The 'Silky' World of Bengal Trade", *Proceedings*. Indian History Congress, 52nd Session, Delhi, 1992.

57d. *Ibratnamah*, Vol. I, p. 19 cited in Humaira Dasti, loc. cit., p. 251

57e. Humaira Dasti, *loc. cit.*, p. 252

58. Fraser, p. 545

59. Badruddin Kashmiri, "Rauzat-ut-Rizwan".

60. Shastitko, p. 14; *Tarikh-i-Manazil-Bukhara*, p. 34.

60a. A.M. Mattoo, "Shawl Industry in Kashmir in The Mughal Period", *Proceedings*. Indian History Congress, Thirty Sixth Session, Aligarh, 1975, p. 270.

61. Vigne, p. 70.

61a. Ya.G. Gulyarmov (ed), *Istoriya Uzbekskoi SSR*, Vol. I, Tashkent, 1967, p. 571.

62. P.E. Matvievskii, "O roli Orenburga v Russko-indiiskoi Torgovle v XVIII v., *"Istoriya SSSR*, No. 3, 1969, p. 105.

63. *Ibid.*, p. 108

64. *Ibid.*

65. *Ibid, loc. cit.*, pp. 108-09

66. *Ibid.*, p. 110

67. *Ibid.*, pp. 108-09

68. *Ibid.*, p. 108; Kazim calculated that Nadir Shah had brought 700 million rupees worth of gold, silver and other valuables from India, Kazim, p. 28.

69. *Ibid.*, p. 110. Another estimate by the same author puts the gold carried by Nadir Shah at 180,00 Kgs. *Ibid.*, p. 153

70. *Ibid.*

71. *Ibid*, pp. 105-06

72. *R-I-O-v XVIII v.*, pp. 342-43

73. P.E. Matvievskii, "Gens i ego Orenburgskaya Zapisi O russko
indiiskikh svyazyakh v XVII-pervoi treti XIX veka," *Iz Istorii Yuzhnoqo
Urala i Za-Urala*, 1966, p. 61

74. *Ibid.*, p. 66, f.n. 1

75. Shastitko, p. 12

76. *Ibid.*, p. 13

77. *Ibid*, p. 14.

78. *R-I-O. v. XVII v.*, no. 173

79. Fraser, pp. 93-94

79a. S.P. Chablani, *Economic Conditions in Sind*, Bombay, 1951, p. 63.
Timur Shah asked them to settle down 'without dread of indefinite
extortion'.

79b. *Ibid.*; K.M. Warikoo, *Central Asia and Kashmir*, New Delhi, 1989,
Ch. 2.

80. Vigne, p. 165

81. *Ibid.*

82. Elphinstone II, p. 264

83. Pottinger, p. 328. Pottinger sent to explore the territory of Baluchistan
and Iran, posed as a horse dealer; See also Fraser, p. 272. He spoke of
Mashad, "Not only the court of Tehran, but most of the nobility in the
western and northern parts of Persia, as well as in Khorasan, are
supplied from this quarter with their most favourite horses; there is
besides a very considerable export to Bokhara, to Candhar, to Cabul.
The Punjab and India; nay there is little doubt that a large proportion
of these horse brought by the Cabul dealers to our Indian provinces
have originally been obtained from Khorasan, and breeding plains
around it."

84. *Ibid.*, 416

85. Elphinstone II, p. 189; *Tarikh-i-Manazil-i-Bukhara*, p. 33.

85a. Mohammad Ashraf Wani, "Transfer of Military Technology from
Central Asia to Kashmir," *The Journal of Central Asian Studies, No.
1. 1992.* p. 72 and f.n. 68.

86. *Tarikh-i-Manazil-i-Bukhara*, p. 33

87. Vigne, p. 69

87a. Humaira Dasti, *loc.cit.*, p. 252.

87b. We have the example of an Indian, Pandu by name visiting the cities of Tobolok, Yeniseisk and Irkutsk in Siberia. He was probably the first Indian to go to Siberia. We have no idea either about the purpose or the place from which he undertook the journey. T.A. Lapteva and M.P. Lukichev, "Documents of the USSR State Archive of Ancient Acts Pertaining to the History of Russian-Indian Relations," *Proceedings*, Indian Historical Records Commission, Vol. LII, Srinagar, 1988, p. 53

88. Yu. Sokolov, p. 52

89. Kazim, pp. 97-98

90. *R-I-O. v, XVIII v,* p. 342

91. Peter Hopkirk, *The Great Game,* OUP, 1991

92. Mattoo, *loc cit.,* p. 42.

3

Indians around the Pamir Plateau in the First Decade of the Nineteenth Century: A View of Contemporary Russians*

Surendra Gopal

By the seventeenth century several European countries had established sea-trade with the Orient especially with India. The Tsarist Russia could not do so because of her geographical location. As the century advanced, she felt increasingly hurt because of her inability to share the profits of Indian and Eastern trade with the Western European nations.

The Russian contacts with India were older than that of the nations of the north-western Europe, be it England, France, or Holland, etc. They had their own distinguishing features. Afanasi Nikitin had visited India in 1469[1] and by 1630s the Indians had appeared in the Russian capital Moscow[2] and its other cities.[3] Soon a colony of Indians emerged in Astrakhan.[4] No Indian colony existed in any other European country such as England, Holland or France, etc., despite their continuously increasing and intensive trade contacts with India. The presence of Indians on the Russian soil further stimulated the Tsarist desire to have direct access to India, Indian commodities and Indian trade.

---

*   P.K. Mishra (ed.), *Aspects of Indian History and Historiogrpahy*, New Delhi, 1996, pp. 203-10.

Aware that they could not reach India by the sea-route because of geographical constraints, the Russian authorities tried to collect authentic and detailed information about India, Indians and routes to India from Indians, from Russian merchants and officers in touch with Indians or working in areas bordering Persia and Central Asia. They appointed envoys to the Mughal court in the hope that they would bring in first-hand information about India. One of these diplomats managed to travel to the peninsular India where the last Great Mughal Emperor Aurangzeb was holding his Court.[5] Diplomatic relations could not be established and the Russian quest for direct access to India through Central Asia/Iran continued.

Peter the Great persisted with this dream in the beginning of the eighteenth century. He decided on a route which would emanate from the shores of the Caspian and the Aral Seas and enable Russian ships to sail down the Oxus river (which emptied into the Aral Sea) and then reach India via Afghanistan.[6]

With this end in view the fortress of Orenburg, established in the Kazakh steppe on the banks of river Ural[7] in 1735, was sought to be developed as a center for trade with Central Asia and further on to India. But here again they did not meet with the expected success. The Russian search for a route to India via Central Asia had now a new dimension.

The Russians in the eighteenth century even tried to find out a sea-route to India but geography thwarted their efforts.[8] Russian entry into the Black Sea at the cost of the Ottoman empire was brought to nought by the European powers who felt Russian competition would threaten their interests.

By the last decade of the eighteenth century political changes in Europe forced Russia to take a new look at their plans for direct trade with India.

The rise of Napoleon Bonaparte in France was an event which invested the world politics with new possibilities.

The French who had challenged British supremacy on the soil of India from 1740s onwards now decided to change their tactics.

Spurred by Tipu's overtures (the ruler of Mysore and an implacable foe of the Britishers), the French decided to forge a joint front with the Russians to invade India via West Asia and Persia.[9] The scheme proved to be a non-starter but made the Britishers conscious of the fact that Persia could be a launching pad for an invasion against their most prized colonial possession, India, by a rival European power. In this case it could well be Russia, now breathing down the necks of the Persians across the Caspian Sea and the Caucusus mountain and already actively engaged in strengthening trade and diplomatic ties with the Central Asian Khanates. The British therefore increased their surveillance of Persia and the Malcolm mission in 1800 was an effort to stall the designs of any non-British European power to attack India from the soil of Iran.[10] After all, they had seen that in 1739 Nadir Shah, the Persian ruler had successfully invaded India and captured the capital city of Delhi.

The pre-emptive move of the British in Iran stimulated Russians to try to develop a new route to India via Central Asian Khanates where the likelihood of British interference were very little. The Russians who had kept alive the issue of the Central Asian route now decided to try one via the Kazakh steppe bordering southern Siberia since their territories almost touched the Chinese-ruled Eastern Turkistan. They felt that a regular route to India could be discovered through Chineses Turkistan i.e. via the cities of Kulja, Kashgar, Yarkand and then on to the Kashmir region of India.

The Russians expected that their entry by this route would not be opposed by the European powers, especially the Britishers, who despite being the dominant power in India did not control the territory from Kashmir to the Arab Sea. The Afghans ruled over Kashmir, the trans-Indian region of the Punjab (till 1793) and Sindh.

Hence, intensive efforts for making the new route operational after bypassing the oft-traversed and widely used route through the kingdom of Bukhara, northeast Iran (i.e. Khurasan) and Afghanistan were started by the Russians.

This started, as we shall see, in course of a couple of decades, colonial rivalry around the Pamir mountains.

The probings were begun by the merchants. Trade and not conquest was projected as the main motive. The selected merchants were not exclusively Russians. They included all those who had been involved with Russians in business dealing in the area of Central Asia, in Orenburg and Astrakhan, viz., the Tatars, the Bukharans, the Armenians, the Jews, etc.[11]

These merchants were picked up for their loyalty, their proficiency in regional languages, their knowledge and long-existing business contacts in the region and of course, for their business and diplomatic skill. It was expected that their reports after business trips would bring in badly needed diplomatic, economic, ethnological, geographical and other relevant information. They were to report on everything they had seen or learnt about the country so that if in future, when a large military operation had to be conducted, the Russians should not be handicapped by the absence of relevant information.

The Russian hopes were not belied. These merchants gave interesting data about the places they visited including an account of the activities of the Indians in the cities of Eastern Turkistan. We also get an idea about the importance of Indian trade and their view on Indian political scene.

The deliberate Russian search for the route to India via Eastern Turkistan was begun by a Georgian merchant Rafail Danibegov,[12] who first went to India towards the end to the eighteenth century and returned via Kashmir, Western China, Tibet and Semiplatinsk. After his second trip to Kashmir, Rafail Danibegov returned in 1807.[13]

While Danibegov was undertaking his second trip to India, Mehti Rafailov, a Georgian Jew, resident in Kabul and having wide commercial interests in the region in the Central Asian Khanates, Badakhshan, Kashmir and Eastern Turkistan, Tibet, etc., also returned after a trip to Kashmir to St. Petersberg via Semiplatinsk.[14] He had brought with him Indian goods worth 'a considerable sum'.

The Russian Foreign Minister N.P. Rumyantsev received him along with two other famous merchants of Semiplatinsk, Madatov and Shargilov. Rumyantsev directed them to undertake a business trip to Western China and Kashmir.[15]   While Mehti Rafailov and Shargilov immediately left for Eastern Turkistan and other countries and returned in 1811,[16] Madatov started on the journey only in 1809.

Madatov spent four years in Kashmir and brought back 250 shawls which after sale fetched him high profits.[17]

The choice of Mehti Rafailov, who basically conducted his business from Kabul and was well-acquainted with the region was also dictated by his linguistic ability. He knew a number of languages spoken widely in the region, Persian, Turkish, Tatar, Punjabi, Kashmiri, etc.[18]

His ancestry is not known. His was a 'rags to riches' story. Some describe him as a Jew from Iran. [19] Whatever be it, Rafailov had created an extensive business empire with its seat in Kabul and was a well known figure in business circles in Afghanistan, in the Trans-Oxus region, in Badakhshan, the Pamir and the adjoining regions of Eastern Turkistan, Tibet and Indian portion of Kashmir and the Punjab.

The Tsarist officials decided to profit by Mehti Rafailov's knowledge and wide acquaintance. He was inducted in a team of four merchants selected for undertaking a journey to Eastern Turkistan, to the adjoining area of Tibet, Kashmir, etc. He was to set out from the fortress of Semiplatinsk which had been set up in 1718,[19] and was a major centre for the departure of caravans of Russian merchants towards Eastern Turkistan.

In the closing decades of the eighteenth century, Semiplatinsk had[20] emerged as a new base of operations for merchants and agents sent by the Russian government to develop trade across the Tien Shan mountains, to the Chinese-held territory, Tibet, India, Kashmir, etc., ostensibly to seek new markets for Russian goods but also to gain valuable geographical, economic, political, social information.

In case the visits helped Russia to establish a reliable and safe route to India, then Russia would be in a position to outflank the British and gain entry into an area in India which was still outside

British domination and therefore, theoretically free from their possible interference.

These motives impelled the Tsar and his officials to send Mehti Rafailov four times.[21] After his return from three visits (he died during the fourth visit which began in 1820 at a place called Kam-Kurom after leaving Yarkand for Tibet)[22] he was asked to submit his report. He was also interrogated by the commander of the Fort of Semiplatinsk. Furthermore the reports and the statement made by Mehti Rafailov were thereafter forwarded to appropriate authorities in the Russian capital, St. Petersberg.

In 1807 Mehti Rafailov, Madatov, Artemov and Shargilov returned from Kashmir after successfully conducting their business with a consignment of shawls. The Russian foreign ministry called them to St. Petersberg and the Foreign Minister N.P. Rumyantsev asked them to proceed once gain and they left Semiplatinsk on 4 August 1808. In course of three years they visited Kulja, Aksu, Kashgar, Yarkand and Kashmir and returned to Semiplatinsk in March 1811.[23]

Rafailov submitted his first report to Glazenag, the local military commander which was forwarded to the Russian Foreign Minister and he was asked to proceed to St. Petersberg along with his goods.[24] Glazenag in his second letter forwarded the detailed account given by Rafailov of the cities and regions which he had visited.

The Report of Rafailov enhanced the confidence of the Russian government in him and convinced them that India could be reached by this route. He was again asked to lead another caravan along with goods worth 110306 roubles and 90 kopecks.[25]

The government had so much confidence in him that he started his visit to the region with goods worth 160,000 roubles and was given a letter for the ruler of Tibet.[26] He intended to go to Kashmir but returned without visiting Kashmir as he was able to sell all his goods and procure Kashmiri goods in 'Tibet'.[27] He returned via Kulja to Semiplatinsk.

For all that he was doing for Russian trade, Rafailov wanted reward and recognition from the Tsar, who made him a commercial counsellor in 1817.[28] In 1819 he was honoured by the Tsar; he was made a Court Counsellor.[29] His stock at the court of St. Petersberg remainted high and he was asked in 1819 to undertake another journey to deliver a letter from the Russian Foreign Minister, Nesselrode to Maharaja Ranjit Singh, the ruler of the Punjab.

This time it was to be more than a commercial expedition. He was to carry a letter for the ruler of 'Tibet'.

The Tsarist government sought an alliance with Ranjit Singh and wanted to develop bilateral trade relations. This letter never reached Ranjit Singh as Rafailov died during his trip before reaching the Punjab.

The Reports of Rafailov shed interesting light on the commercial activities of Indians in the region of Eastern Turkistan and Tibet, the importance of the trade and the routes that the traders followed.

In the report which Rafailov submitted after completing the first trip in 1808, he says that in the city of Ask or Aksu, he found merchants from Tashkent, Bukhara, Kashmir, India and also the 'wild Kirghizs'.[30] All the merchants were taxed at the rate of 'one piece out of thirty' and 'one animal out of thirty' but the Kashmiris were required to pay 'one piece out of forty-one' and 'one animal out of forty-one'.[31]

Obviously there was a long tradition of the Kashmiri and Indian merchants undertaking this long and arduous trip to Aksu, otherwise they would not have been given these concessions. Probably this was the northern most point reached by them. We do not get any idea of the religious persuasion of these Kashmiri and Indian merchants.

The road to Aksu from Kashmir ran through the intervening areas of Ladakh, Yarkand and Kashgar.

Yarkand was another city frequented by traders from Kashmir. In course of a subsequent visit to the city in 1813, Rafailov met with a Kashmiri merchant from whom he purchased Kashmiri shawls and spent all the money he had.[32] As a result, he had to cancel his proposed visit to Kashmir since his requirements had been met and he had no more money to invest.

The Kashmiri merchant was prepared to visit Russia in his company but had to give up the project as he was called back to Kashmir.

We come across another interesting fact: Rafailov after Yarkand fails to identify a place by its name. He describes the places by the name of the region to which they belonged. Thus Leh in Ladakh and other contiguous places are described as Tibet all through. When he left Ladakh and entered the Kashmir valley, he does not mention the name of any city. All through he gives his impression in terms of the region. The description shows how rudimentary the knowledge of the geography of this region was among the Russians and also among the merchants visiting this area of Ladakh and the Kashmir valley.

He speaks of Tibet. We are not clear about the exact place he visited. But it seems he was referring to Ladakh.[33]

It took him thirty-four days to reach Ladakh.[34] From Yarkand to Ladakh, a distance of about 100 versts was flat but thereafter he crossed several mountains, Karakuram (Black stone), Muzdaban (mountain of snow), Karaul Dabam (mountain of watchmen), Aktan (white mountain), Karatan (black mountain) and Kizyltan (red mountain). These mountain ranges were very high and 'some of them were perpetually covered by snow'. There were hardly any forests. Those that existed lay along small rivers and were met only after a day's or two journey. There was no grass and hence travellers carried 'barley and fodder for their horses'.[35]

According to him the entire area between Yarkand and 'Tibet' was full of mountains and was uninhabited.

The 'city of Tibet' was free, not subservient to any power: the ruler was called 'Raja'.

The people of 'Tibet' professed a religion which believed in idol-worship. They were Buddhists.

There were very few villages around 'The City' and there was very little cultivation because of unavailability of cultivable land.

The air was heavy and harmful. As a result, according to Rafailov, the people were weak and did not have a good colour on the face. The local people agreed that the climate of the land where they lived was not healthy.

The city itself was economically in a very bad shape. It was economically sustained because of the export of valuable wool to Kashmir. Similarly, the people earned some money because of the visits of traders from 'Kashmir, Hasa, Yarkand and India'.[36]

The wool was purchased by Kashmiris for the manufacture of shawl. The quantum of wool thus sold amounted to 7000 poods each year.

The government charged customs duties from traders who passed through the city. The local residents arranged for the stay of the traders in their houses.

The people were not war-like. According to Rafailov 'they did not know even the meaning of war'.[37]

Rafailov left for Kashmir after staying for eight days in Ladakh and after obtaining a pass-port from the local ruler.

The journey to Kashmir took seventeen days and he passed seventeen villages. Up to the place 'Drast', the people belonged to the Tibetan race and thereafter they were all Kashmiris.

The people in general were poor; they were either farmers or were engaged in animal-husbandry. Each place contained from 20 to 30 houses.

The route from 'Tibet' to Kahsmir was hilly, full of forests, cultivated land and plenty of orchards.

He correctly stated that the valley was under the sovereignty of the Afghans but on account of the civil war raging among them, 'the local governor withheld the payment of the annual tribute of 15,000,000 roubles'.[38] The figure was only a guess-work.

Then he goes on to say that this region was divided into two by the 'river Vernak'.[39]

The valley had a number of cities which had '1,00,000 houses'; out of which '20,000 houses' belonged to 'people of the Indian law'.[40] He obviously means non-Muslims, i.e., Hindus.

The houses were small, each meant for only one family and these could not be compared to the large European houses.

The population here consisted of people from 'Turkey, Persia, India, Afghanistan, Yarkand and Bukhara'. Rafailov's observation was perfectly correct in this regard as merchants from all the adjoining regions frequented the Kashmir valley.

Without naming the chief city in the valley, he went on to say that it had '20,000 looms'.[41] The government received an income of '1,200,000 roubles' from taxes levied on them.[42]

The city itself was not fortified. But the place where the governor lived was surrounded by a brick-wall. The army consisted of cavalry, numbering between ten and twelve thousand and infantry between eight and ten thousand. They had fire-arms but 'these were locally made after the Asian fashion and were without locks into wicks'.[43]

The majority of the Kashmiris were Muslims and some of them professed the 'Indian faith', i.e. Hinduism.[44]

The cities and other areas of Kashmir were surrounded by high mountains.

The people of the country were 'beautiful, healthy, clever and enterprising'. They were hospitable.[45]

There were no factories for making any variety of metal.

The local authorities charged the same customs duties on all goods either imported or exported by the merchants.[46]

They did not charge any duty on either the import or export of gold and silver.[47]

Rafailov returned to Semiplatinsk from Kashmir by the same route by which he came. In all he calculated the distance to be 2010 versts to be covered in sixty-seven days.[48]

He described this route running through the towns of 'small Bukhara' i.e. Eastern Turkistan as the best because one could easily find food and also because there was peace and 'no disquiet' among the local populations.[49]

He was keen that Russia should bring all these areas under its protection.[50] He averred that the task was easy as the 'Chinese authorities lacked courage'.[51]

After subsequent visit in 1813 to Kashmir Rafailov presented another detailed account of the various routes which could be taken by the merchants going from Russia to India.

He also analysed the political situation in the area. His aim was to assure the Tsarist authorities that the advance of the Russians would be welcomed and the local rulers would submit to the protection afforded by the Tsar. He dangled the hope of large profits accruing from the unhindered and increased trade with the region.

In a subsequent note on the routes to India which were fairly detailed he again dwelt upon the importance of Indian trade and the activities of the Indian traders in the area.

For example, when he wrote in detail about Ladakh (called by him 'Tibet'), he clearly stated that the route from Bukhara to Kashmir lay through Ladakh. The Raja, out of fear for the might of the ruler of Kashmir and also because of the advantages he gained as a result of transit trade passing via the territory to Kashmir, submitted to the governor of Kashmir.[52] His income consisted solely of customs duties imposed on caravans passing through his territory and on fine wool carried by the Kashmiris for the manufacture of shawls and other wooleen clothes.

He pointed out that the Ladakhis knew nothing about warfare and did not possess fire-arms. The ruler of Kashmir who kept friendly ties with the Ladakhi ruler, however, would not come to his aid in the event of any external attack.[53]

Rafailov was very clear about the fact that the roots of prosperity of Kashmir lay in Ladakh since three-fourth of the Kashmiris was engaged in weaving shawls and other woollen garments and one-fourth earned profits from selling them.[54] The wool came from Ladakh.

Rafailov was sure that if Russia extended its hands of friendship to the Sikh ruler of the Punjab, he would welcome it.[55] He expressed the fear that Britishers, who had already occupied a major portion of India, were preparing in the near future to extinguish the freedom of the Punjab.[56] He even mentioned Delhi, the fate of the Marathas, who had been driven out by the Britishers.

Rafailov suggested that imperial Russian authorities should enter into correspondence and establish friendly relations with 'the Afghans, the Marathas and the successors of Tipoo Sultan'.[57] Obviously impressed by the description and analysis of the prevailing political and economic situation, the imperial Russian authorities entrusted him with a letter for Maharaja Ranjit Singh. As stated earlier, Rafailov died in course of the journey before reaching the Punjab and the letter could never be delivered.

Rafailov's accounts of his journeys and the circumstances surrounding it clearly show that the imperial Russian authorities were extremely keen to establish stable trade contacts with India by the overland route even though it meant bypassing the oft-used road running through Bukhara, Balkh, Kabul, Peshawar, etc., if that was feasible in spite of the barriers of high mountains surrounding Ladakh and Kashmir and the barren terrain through which it ran. The caravans carrying merchandise would be, in future, escorted by armed contingents if such a course suggested itself after the failure of diplomatic overture.

The Russian advances drew appropriate response on the part of the British authorities safely ensconced on the Indian sub-continent. The 'Great Game on High Pamirs' now began.

The Malcolm mission was the precursor of a series of diplomatic missions and agents in the guise of merchants or travellers were sent by the British throughout the century to gauge the Russian designs. Like the Russians they also used local Indians (both Hindus and Muslims).[59]

To justify their actions the British portrayed the growing Russian interest as directed against the 'jewel in the crown'. For the whole of the nineteenth century, British policy in India was determined and influenced by Russo-phobia.

The search for markets culminated in imperial and colonial rivalry which in the nineteenth century wrote the history of Central Asia, Eastern Turkistan, Tibet and other adjoining regions of India.

REFERENCES

1. Khalfin, N.A. and Shastitko, P.M.(eds) *Rossiya i Indiya*, Moskva, 1980, p.35. Some scholars believe that Nikitin arrived in India in 1471.

2. Goldberg N.M.(ed).) *Russko-Indiiskiye Otnosheniya V XVIII v.*, Moskva, 1958(henceforth cited as R.I-O V XVIII v.)

3. *Ibid.*, Doc. no.38.

4. Yukht, A.I., "Indiiskaya koloniya v Astrakhani," *Voprosy Istorii*, 1957, No.3.

5. In the seventeenth century the Tsars sent four diplomatic missions to India. *Rossiya i Indiya*, p.45; *Ibid.*, p. 63. Aurangzeb received the Russian envoy Semen Malenki.

6. *Rossiaya i Indiya*, pp. 75-76.

7. The river falls into the Caspian Sea.

8. *Rossiya i Indiya*, p. 77; K.A. Antonova (ed), *R.I-O. V XVII v.*, Moskva, 1965 Docs. 175-77.

9. Hopkirk, Peter, *The Great Game*, OUP, 1991, pp.21, 26, 27.

10. Hopkirk, pp.31-2.
11. *Rossiya i Indiya*, pp. 80, 98, 99.
12. *Rossiya i Indiya,* p. 101. He thrice went to India.
13. *Ibid.* 'During, his third journey (1822-23) he spent 'five years in India', He returned via-Lahore, Kashmir, Kabul and Bukhara to Orenburg and dictated his memoirs, *Ibid.*
14. *Ibid.*, p 101.
15. *Ibid.*
16. Shastitko, P.M. (ed), *Rossiskiye puteshestveniki v indii v XIX-nachalo XX v,* Moskva, 1990, p.14.
17. *Rossiya i Indiya,* p. 101.
18. *Rossiiskiye.*, pp. 15,16
19. *Ibid.*, p. 14. *Rossiya i Indiya*, p.12.
20. *Rossiskiye* ..., p.14.
21. *Rossiya i Indiya,* pp. 101-102,
22. *Rossiskiye* ..., p.22. His companion Mohammed Zugur, however, reached Kashmir and spent there ten months and purchased shawls and spent all the money left by Rafailov.
23. *Rossiskiye*..., p.14.
24. *Ibid.*
25. *Ibid.*, p.15.
26. *Ibid.*, p.18.
27. *Ibid.*, p. 19.
28. *Ibid.*, p. 20.
29. *Ibid.*
30. *Rossiskiya*...., p. 33.
31. *Ibid.*, p. 33.
32. *Ibid.*, p. 75.
33. *Ibid.*, p. 35, f.n. 10.
34. *Ibid.*, 35.
35. *Ibid.*, p. 35.
36. *Ibid.*, p. 35.
37. *Ibid.*
38. *Ibid.*, p. 35.
39. *Ibid.*, p. 36.

40. *Ibid.*
41. *Ibid.*
42. *Ibid.*
43. *Ibid.*, p. 36.
44. *Ibid.*
45. *Ibid.*
46. *Ibid.*, p. 36.
47. *Ibid.*
48. *Ibid.* p. 39.
49. *Ibid.*
50. *Ibid.*, p. 40.
51. *Ibid.*
52. *Ibid.*, p. 44.
53. *Ibid.*
54. *Ibid.*, p. 44.
55. *Ibid.*, p. 44-45.
56. *Ibid.*, p. 45.
57. *Ibid.*, p. 45.
58. Shastitko "Missiya Mekhti Rafailova k Ranjit Singhu, *Sovetskoye Vostokotedeniye,* 1957, No.4.
59. Indian agents such as Meer Izzatullah and Hafiz Mohammed Fazil Khan had been sent. Later on, Moorcroft went to Leh and Kashmir. He could not journey to Yarkand, Hopkirk, pp. 92-95. He was in Leh when Rafailov unexpectedly died. He reported the event to his superiors in Calcutta.

4

The Economic Relations between India and Central Asia in the 19th Century*

Devendra Kaushik

The Mughals in India might not have succeeded in incorporating Central Asia, their homeland, into their Empire, but this did not prevent the regular flow of commerce and trade through the overland caravan routes. During Akbar's reign two caravan routes to Central Asia were in regular use—one from Lahore to Kabul and the other from Multan to Kandhar. Bukhara, Samarkand, Khiva, and Merv in Central Asia remained in regular contact with such important Indian trade centres as Peshawar, Shikarpur, Multan and Lahore all through the medieval period of history.

During the nineteenth century Central Asia was linked with India through four overland caravan routes. Three of these routes passed through Afghanistan and one led to Central Asia through Kashmir, Ladakh and the Sinkiang province of China also known as Eastern or Chinese Turkistan. The most common route was from Lahore, Peshawar through the Khyber pass to Kabul (to Kabul came another branch-route from the town of Dera Ismail Khan in the upper Indus valley through the Gomal pass and Ghazni Plateau). From Kabul this route led to Central Asia via Bamian, Tashkurgan, Mazar-i-Sharif and then across the Amu river at Kelif into the territory of the

---

*   Devendra Kaushik, *India and Central Asia in Modern Times*, New Delhi, 1985, pp. 66-80.

Bukharan Khanate terminating in Bukhara through Karshi. The second route started from Karachi in the south and proceeded along the Indus to the town of Shikarpur and further through the Bolan Pass to Kandhar and Herat. From Herat this route reached Central Asia through Mashad in Persia joining Ashkhabad. The Third route to Central Asia also passed through Herat joining it with Merv.

A flourishing trade existed between India and Central Asia in the early nineteenth century. Meer Izzut-oolah who travelled to Bukhara in 1812-13 wrote: "Into Bukhara is imported from Peshawar, Cabul and Shikarpur, woollen cloth, turbans, white cotton cloth, chintz, molasses, sugar, turmeric, pepper and books of Mahomedan theology and law."[1] He also testified to the Hindu merchants of Shikarpur issuing drafts on their firms or local agents charging 20 to 25 per cent.[2] Alexander Burnes who followed Izzut-oolah to Bukhara in the 1830s gave more detailed account of Indian trade with Central Asia. According to him the demand for Indian goods in Bukhara was "steady". His estimate of the volume of Indian trade with Bukhara was 1,000 camel-load, which was the same as with Kabul.[3] Among the articles exported to Bukhara from India, Burnes mentions Dacca muslin and Banaras brocade (500 pieces annually). The Russians who also imported Indian brocade developed an imitation brocade looking nearly like the stuff from Banaras, which they exported to Bukhara.[4]

Burnes observed: "The whole of the natives of Bukhara and Turkistan wear turbans of white cloth which are imported from the Punjab."[5] These turbans about thirty yards long and a foot broad were worn by both men and women and sold for one *tilla* each. Burnes' remark that such turbans "might be manufactured in Europe and sent with advantage into Toorkistan" reveals the British ire at the flourishing Indian trade with Central Asia. Another star-item of Indian trade was the Kashmiri shawls of which 120 to 300 pieces worth two lakhs of rupees passed to Russia in 1832.[6] Burnes also wrote about the "great passion for shawls among the Russian nobles", which accounted for their exorbitant prices. The item which occupied the most important place among the Bukharan imports from India was indigo (500 camel-loads a year according to Burnes' account).[7] In the year 1833, the import of Indian indigo was estimated at even 1,000 camel-loads.[8] Russian traveller N. Khanykov's estimate of Indian exports to Central Asia in the 1840s was 3,000 to 3,500 camel-loads.[9]

India's trade with Bukhara continued to be brisk even after the annexation of a part of Central Asia by the Tsarist Russia in the mid 1860s. In 1868, 6,500 camel-loads of Indian goods consisting of 65 to 100 thousand *puds* of tea (one *pud* was equal to sixteen kilograms) and 500 camel-loads of manufactured goods reached Bukhara.[10] Thus, in about thirty-five years that elapsed since Burnes' visit to Bukhara the volume of trade with India expanded more than six times from one thousand to six thousand five hundred camel-loads. Bukhara exported to India, through Afghanistan, silk, horses, hashish, and goat's hair. The silk exported to India was mostly brought to Bukhara from the neighbouring Kokand Khanate which was famous for producing silk. Among the silk-made articles from Bukhara were table cloths and scarfs. In all, six thousand *puds* of such articles and 800 bundles of silk were annually exported to India.[11] Yet the exports of Bukhara to India remained insignificant. Even by the end of the 1880s their relative share in the total Bukharan exports was very low. In a total of 15 million roubles worth of export trade of Bukhara the share of India was less than 0.5 million (Russian 12.5 million and Persia 2.12 million roubles.)[12]

The Indian exports to Bukhara in the 1870s and 1880s consisted of tea (70 thousand *puds*), indigo (18 thousand *puds*), brocades (about 300 pieces) annually.[13] The unsettled conditions in Afganistan, however, adversely affected the Central Asian trade with India, which passed through that country. The trade volume between Afghanistan and India fell between 15-20 per cent during the period 1881-1884 due to internal disturbances. Amir Abdur Rahman Khan who was earlier well disposed towards the transit trade through his kingdom, began to impose greater restrictions on it in the later years of his rule. All this led to a search for a better and safer route for trade with India.

The route through Bandar Abbas, Mashad, Herat and Karki was found to be more attractive at a time when the revolt of tribes in northern Afghanistan created dangerous conditions for transit trade passing through that area. But as the Bandar Abbas-Mashad route through Persia was twice longer than the route through Kabul, the latter still continued to be important. In 1891, 44,000 *puds* of tea worth 1,760 thousand roubles and 160,544 pieces of muslin worth 418 thousand roubles were brought through Kabul to Bukhara as compared to 53,495 *puds* of tea worth 1,667 thousand roubles, indigo, 4,697 thousand *puds* worth 164 thousand roubles and 48,480 pieces of muslin worth 104 thousand roubles received through the Persian route. The total amount of trade through Afghanistan and Persia was estimated at 2,178 thousand and 1,935 thousand roubles respectively.[14]

The Farghana-Kashgar-Kashmir route was not very popular until after the inclusion of entire Central Asia into a common Russian tariff system in 1894. The route through the Kanjut territory joining Central Asia through Vakhan and Hindukush passes which the British authorities in India had improved considerably could have been a shorter and more convenient route, but it was closed by the British due to strategic considerations. The British developed the other route through Leh and a considerable trade with Kashgar and the Russian Turkistan appears to have flowed through this route in the 1890s. Russian traveller, V.F. Novitskii who returned to Farghana through the Kashmir-Kashgar route met a number of Indian merchants from Shikarpur in the different towns of Eastern Turkistan. These merchants who lived side by side with many Central Asian merchants were engaged in a brisk trade between India and Central Asia through Kashgar and Kashmir.[15] Russian manufactured goods captured the entire market of Eastern Turkistan and extended their sway even up to Chitral on account of their cheapness in comparison to British manufactured goods, wrote Logofet.[16] According to A.F. Gubarevich-Radobylskii, by the end of the last century the turnover of Indian trade with Kashgar had been reduced to the insignificant amount of just about two million roubles and many of the Indian merchants living in Kashgar had taken to trade in Russian commodities.[17]

But if the Russian goods had driven out, towards the end of the last century, the British manufactured goods from the markets of Chinese or Eastern Turkistan, trade in the latter picked up in Central Asia after the construction of the Trans-Caucasian railway linking the Black Sea port of the Poti with Baku on the Caspian Sea through Tbilisi. From Baku the British-Indian goods were transported across the Caspian to Astrabad, reaching Central Asia through Mashad.

The Russian bourgeoisie aspired to acquire a dominant position in the Central Asian market for which it waged a long struggle against the Indian traders. Indian and Kokand merchants petitioned against Russian merchants to the Military Governor of Syr-Darya district complaining that they were causing delay in the examination of their goods with Tashkent as destination.[18] Beginning with April 1868, the Russian administration began to place restrictions on the import of indigo and on 22 April 1868 the import of indigo and muslin from India was taxed at par with foreign goods entering Russia from across its European borders. Indian tea was, however, not to be charged customs duty at the rate payable for goods entering from the side of European borders; it had to pay only a surcharge of 5 per cent over the traditional *Zakat* tax levied at the rate of one-fortieth part of its cost.[19] Import of all other British-Indian goods except indigo, muslin and tea was temporarily prohibited in Turkistan.

But even these restrictions had little effect on the volume of Indian goods entering Central Asia. Indian goods freely reached Khiva and Bukhara and continued to penetrate into Russian Turkistan through Bukharan traders who had free access to this market. An official estimate of Bukhara's trade with India in 1893 put it at 112 thousand *puds* of tea, 28 thousand *puds* of indigo and 20 thousand *puds* of muslin.[20] To meet this situation the all-Russian Customs Union was extended to Bukhara and Khiva in 1894. Under the new regulations only the import of indigo, precious stones, white muslin and tea was permitted on payment of a special customs duty. Black tea was charged at the rate of 25 roubles per *pud* and green tea at 15 roubles, 40 copeck.[21] This was changed to a uniform duty of 12 roubles per *pud* in 1901, which was raised to 18 roubles in 1915.[22]

The 1894 Law did make a dent in the Peshawari merchant's monopoly of tea trade with Central Asia. A part of this trade now began to pass into the hands of the Russian merchants. But the opening of the new sea and railway route through the Trans-Caucasian railway from the Black Sea port of Batumi to Baku on the Caspian Sea and the Trans-Caspian railway from Krasnovodsk on the other side of the Caspian Sea reduced the transport cost and enabled the Indian merchants to compete with the Russian merchants for the tea trade in Central Asia. The number of Indian traders in Bukhara engaged in tea trade rose from about ten in the 1880s to eighty-three in 1911.[23] In Bukhara the Indian merchants regained, in the 1890s, their lost position in tea trade in Turkistan by supplying tea on long-term credit. In 1896 out of fifty Indian merchants living in Tashkent ten were reported to be engaged in tea trade.[24] In Samarkand in the early years of the twentieth century ten Peshawari firms were doing business in tea; more important among them were the firms of Fazl-i-Ahmadov, Shamsuddinov and Ilahi Bakhsh.[25] Indian Peshawari merchants bought Chinese green tea from Shanghai through the Peshawari firm of Karimbakhsh and some even through Russian firms like Molchanov, Pechatnov and Co., Tokmakov, Molotkov and Co. in Hankow. From China, tea was brought on Russian ships to Batumi and sold in Central Asia as Indian tea. Some black and green tea produced in India was also brought by Indian merchants. From 129 thousand *puds* of Indian tea (including the tea from China brought by Indian merchants) imported by Central Asia between 1896 and 1900 the quantity increased to about 597 thousand *puds* in 1911-1912.[26]

It is not correct to say that the Indian merchants did not buy anything in return for sending back to their home in India. Silk was more or less regularly exported by them to India. According to Gubarevich-Radobylskii, about 2,000 *puds* of silk were annually exported to India from Bukhara.[27] An Indian Peshawari merchant purchased 4,000 Uzbek gowns in 1888. Some carpets were also exported to India through Indian merchants.[28] One Peshawari merchant Fazle Ilahi sent to India thirty-two bundles of Russian manufactured goods including twenty-two bundles of crockery. Indian merchants also carried Russian goods to Kashgar. In 1909 one of them took there ten thousand roubles worth of Russian cloth.[29] Central Asian exports to India including manufactured goods from Russia had a turnover of 800 thousand roubles in the early years of the twentieth century.[30] Russian boxes (*Sanduks* with metal work), teapots and cups in bright colours and samovars were quite popular in north-western regions of India and in Kashmir. Russian textiles, particularly designed to suit oriental tastes had also a limited demand in these regions. Russian publicists pleaded for a careful study of the Indian market in order to expand further the trade in Russian goods from Central Asia.[31] The Russian Consul-General in Bombay, in a letter published in the *Times of India*, indicated the goods which Russia could supply to India cheaper than any other country and also mentioned Indian goods which could find a market in his country.[32] Kerosene and sugar were also being imported into India from Russia. From 1905 a Russian Consulate started functioning in Bombay.

In the wake of the Anglo-Russian Convention of 1907 which resolved many questions aggravating rivalry between the two colonial powers over Central Asia in the past, the demand for linking Central Asia with India through railroad construction was repeatedly raised in the Russian press. Thus, the *Tashkentskii Kurier* reported A.E. Snesarev's demand for linking Central Asia with India by rail. This demand was voiced by the Russian orientalist in his address to the Society for Indological Studies.[33] The completion of a railway project linking Central Asia with India was described in the Russian press of Central Asia as the realization of the dream of Peter the Great of opening a route to India. General Annenkov, tne constructor of the Trans-Caspian railway, favoured a rail link between Kushka and Chaman through Herat, which, in his opinion, was preferable to the other rail route through Kabul for topographical reasons and economic prospects.[34]

It was argued in the columns of the Central Asian press that the railway link would be advantageous to all the three countries concerned (including Afghanistan). The *Turkestanskie Vedomosti* concurred with the view expressed by the *Pioneer Mail* of India that the project linking India with Russia through Afghanistan by rail should be implemented only with the free consent of Afghanistan. It further wrote that this project could materialize without inviting any criticism only when the Amir had himself built railways in his kingdom.

As already noted, Indian settlements arose in many of the towns of Central Asia long before the incorporation of Turkistan into the Tsarist Russian Empire. Many of these Indian settlers, particularly those from Shikarpur, were actively engaged in moneylending business along with their trading activities. Indian moneylenders mostly advanced small amounts in loan to poor Central Asian peasants and craftsmen. Only in rare cases the credit offered by them amounted to more than one hundred roubles, the majority of the transactions being limited to ten to twenty-five roubles.[35] But they occasionally financed well-to-do merchants as well.[36] According to the testimony of Aini, only those who could not get loan elsewhere came to them.[37] As a rule, loans were advanced under mortgage against property or valuables. V. Nalivkin and M. Nalivkina describe how Indian moneylenders advanced against valuables a sum of sixteen *tenegs* (equal to 3 roubles 20 copecks) and by charging a weekly instalment of one *teneg* realized both the principal and interest over a period of twenty weeks.[38] The Russian paper *Novoye Vremya* published from St. Petersburg condemned Indian moneylenders for cheating their ignorant Central Asian clients and getting their property auctioned even when they had made full payment.[39]

L. Kostenko wrote from Tashkent in the *Golos* No. 88 of 1869 that Indian moneylenders played the same role as Jews in the western part of the Empire and observed that "though hated and suppressed they have nonetheless acquired a great weight with the help of their capital and control all financial transactions in the region." Hungarian traveller, Vambery who visited Central Asia in the 1860s affirmed that there was no market, no village without a Hindu moneylender.[40] Russian authors connected with the Turkistan administration have described Indian moneylenders in the darkest colours. Thus V.V. Krestovskii called them "callous", "worse than even jews" and compared them to "vampires"[41] L.I. Geier writing in the first decade of the twentieth century, described all Indians as moneylenders charging exorbitant rates of interest on the small amounts loaned by them.[42] Archival records confirm incidents of attacks on Indian moneylenders and even their murders on account of hatred against them.[43]

Yet the accounts of Indian moneylenders' operations given by Russian authors close to the administration must not be accepted uncritically for these are in many respects obviously exaggerated. There was hardly any difference in the *modus operandi* of the Indian moneylenders and their counterparts, the Uzbek *bais*, of whom there were many in the credit market. According to G.L. Dmitriyev, in 1903 in the Farghana district alone the Kazis registered credit transactions of local moneylenders with as many as 129,924 persons, that is, one-third of the entire adult population.[44] The administration's hostile approach to Indian moneylenders was also politically motivated. The Russian bourgeoisie, as Dmitriev rightly observes, was only too eager to drive out foreign elements which contended with it for control over the Central Asian economy and market. Moreover, hostile actions against Indian moneylenders were calculated to increase its popularity with the local people. The information given by such former colonial official as Kostenko, Kushakevich, Khoroshkhin, Maev and Arendarenko that most of the Indians living in Central Asia followed the profession of moneylending must be taken with caution. Many Indians were engaged in trade, agriculture and crafts and it would be wrong to associate all of them with the nefarious profession of moneylending.

The absence of any special credit institutions in Central Asia and the continually growing need of the poor peasants and artisans for credit pushed them further into the clutches of Indian moneylenders. The moneylending business got a big boost during the times of acute economic hardship caused by crop failure. Indian moneylenders took advantage of the bad crop years 1870-1871 and stored grain which they then advanced as loan to the local peasants after making them sign the necessary documents, etc. Even with six years of good harvest the peasants of the Zeravshan district (Samarkand) remained indebted to the Indian moneylenders for the debts contracted in 1870 when they had suffered from crop failure.[45] The Indian moneylenders advanced eight *puds* of grain at sowing time and realized sixteen *puds* at harvest time after four months. Thus the loan advanced multiplied five times in just ten months.

G.A. Arendarenko's investigations into the role of Indian moneylenders in the Zeravashan (Samarkand) district which led to the adoption of first legal steps against them deserve a special mention. According to his calculation, on an average an Indian moneylender derived a net profit of 1,700 roubles per year and in this manner all the 375 Indians living in the Zeravashan district earned 637,500 roubles per annum. The Indian moneylenders, according to his information, normally returned to India staying in Central Asia for a period of six years. The entire sum carried home by them in gold in six years was calculated by him at 3,225,000 roubles. The share pocketed by Indian moneylenders from the income of the entire population in the Zeravashan district amounted to 15.5 per cent[46].

The findings of Arendarenko led the Turkistan administration to take strong measures against the Indian merchants. The Governor-General of Turkistan, General Kaufman, sent a circular to the district administrator of the region on 27 October 1877 for "curbing the exploitation of the native population by Indian immigrants".[47] These first steps began to show results in the early 1880s. Thus in Tashkent where before the issue of this circular there were 153 Indians carrying on moneylending activities in 1877; their number declined to 53 in 1882. Even these remaining moneylenders were supervising the liquidation of the credit transactions of either their masters or relations.[48] According to Arendarenko only twenty Indian moneylenders were left in the Zeravashan district by 1882, the rest having wound up their business had gone back home.[49] In 1881 the

Central Asian Commercial Bank was founded with a capital of 500,000 roubles. Soon this bank opened its branches at many places in the region. Indian moneylenders, however, continued to be active in Bukhara as before.

In 1893 the Governor-General of Turkistan, Vrevskii issued a circular ordering the expulsion from Turkistan territory of all Indians carrying on moneylending business and residing without possessing national passports. However, apprehending opposition by the British government, the Governor-General recommended the granting of right to reside without national passports to such citizens of the neighbouring Khanates, Afghanistan and India as did not indulge in moneylending operations. But Vrevskii reserved the right of the Governor-General to expel those Indians whose stay in the region was considered to be harmful.[50]

By 1896 no Indian moneylenders were left in Tashkent which had eighty-three in 1875. I.I. Geier wrote in the early years of the present century that many Indians had completely left moneylending business and taken to trade.[51] In Bukhara this movement of Indians from moneylending to trade was rather quite slow and many Hindu moneylenders continued in their profession until the popular revolution took place in 1920.

G.L. Dmitriyev refers to several Indian merchants adopting the profession of middlemen and agents of the Russian industrial entrepreneurs after the incorporation of a part of Central Asia into the Russian Empire. The records preserved in the state Archives of Uzbekistan mention one Indian resident Paraman Lagurinov who supplied grapes for Tashkent wine factories. In 1897 Bai Bala Gulev supplied to Russian factory owner, N.A. Ivanov, ten thousand *puds* of grapes for 5,000 roubles.

Indian merchants not only acted as middlemen for the Russian industrialists, they also took part in setting up industrial units in Central Asia either independently or jointly with the Russian businessmen. Thus the same Indian Bai Bala Gulev founded a cotton-ginning factory in the village called Mashad near Namangan in the

Farghana district in partnership with Epifanov, a Russian industrialist. This factory had four gins and used steam engines.[52] In Andijan there was another cotton-ginning factory owned by an Indian Peshawari merchant, Yakub Sheikh Nur Khanov, with six gins and two presses.[53] Nur Khanov later on became a Russian citizen. Several Indians like Fazle Ahmadov, Shamsuddin and Ilahi Bakhsh had their own factories in Samarkand for packing tea, with ten to thirty hired workers.[54] Many Indians were employed in these factories as simple workers or office workers.

Some Indians are mentioned by Russian explorers as cultivating land in the Zeravashan district. A few names of Indian grain-growers also figure in archival records which mention names like Ram Das Kishnu, Nukra Bai, and Gopal Singh. According to G.L. Dmitriyev, a Soviet decree of land and water reform from 16 December 1926 also mentions Indians among the national minorities eligible for receiving land through redistribution.[55] Archival records scanned by him also indicate the presence of Indian craftsmen in Central Asia, such as Chetram Mingraj, a bookbinder in Tashkent and Mohan Jitaev, a beltmaker in old Margellan. One Tillya Narchad in Andijan was making dyes for ladies eyebrows. Some Indian barbers, distillers and sweet-makers are also mentioned as carrying their trade in Central Asia. As already mentioned, some Indians practised medicine and treated even many Russians. Indian druggists' (*attar*) shops were functioning in Bukhara, Chardjui and Kattakurgan. American traveller, Eugene Schuyler writes about "the thousand objects of the so-called *Attar* trade (dye-stuffs and drugs)"[56] brought to Bukhara from India in the 1870s.

Indian traders also took an active part in the export trade of Turkistan and the Central Asian Khanates with the neighbouring Afghanistan and Kashgar. They occasionally took back to India large consignments of raw silk, Russian ceramics and manufactured articles. Indian traders played an important role in the trade transactions between the Turkistan region and the Central Asian Khanates. Their role was particularly significant in the Turkistan region's trade with the Khanate of Kokand in the 1860s and 1870s.

From Kokand Indian traders brought to Tashkent, cotton and handmade cloth, Kashgar silk, wool and textile goods, carpets, dressing gowns and dyes, etc., and carried back to Kokand, Russian iron and textile goods, copper, steel, sugar, etc. They also traded in agricultural products like foodgrains, cotton and wool. Some Indians were also engaged in peddling from village to village. Several of them had regular business links with firms in central Russia and participated in trade fairs in the southern Russian cities.[57]

To sum up, the economic relations between India and Central Asia continued to exist notwithstanding the numerous obstacles created in their way by the two colonial powers, Britain and Tsarist Russia, which tried to cordon off their colonial possessions in order to establish an exclusive monopoly over their markets. The restrictions first imposed by Tsarist authorities on the entry of Indian goods into Turkistan in 1868, which were reinforced by the new customs regulations adopted in 1881 and 1894, did deliver a serious blow to the economic relations between the two regions. If these restrictions did not have the desired effect of driving out the Indian trade from Central Asia, it was due to various factors which had nothing to do with the subjective desire of the Tsarist administration. The fear of arousing a hostile reaction among the leading world powers prevented Tsarist Russia from annexing the Khanates of Bukhara and Khiva. The semi-independent status of these Khanates and the opening of the Trans-Caucasian transit route closed only in 1881 enabled the British-Indian goods to reach the Central Asian market. The reduced cost of transport by sea and rail-road somehow helped Indian goods to compete with the Russian goods in the Central Asian market even after 1894 when the Khanates were incorporated into a single customs union for the whole of the Tsarist Empire.

The tenacity of the demand for certain Indian goods among the people of Central Asia as also the ingenuity and resourcefulness of the Indian merchants helped sustain the economic relations between the two regions. However, except for tea and indigo, other Indian goods lost their market in Central Asia and Russian goods acquired an upper hand there. In the case of tea, even while the Indian exports continued to increase in terms of value and quantity, the overall share of Indian tea in the market of Central Asia had fallen and control of its trade by the Peshawari merchants was already a thing of the past. Indian moneylenders' activities were also largely curbed at least in Turkistan by the various administrative and legal measures adopted by the Russian authorities during the last two decades of the nineteenth century. The colonial athorities felt concerned over a serious erosion of the limited capacity of the Central Asian peasants to pay taxes and revenue on account of their heavy indebtedness to foreign moneylenders. The British too were not interested in promoting the export of Indian goods to Central Asia by Indian merchants. Indian tea was taken to London by British merchants and a part of it found its way to Russia through auction sales there. Besides, the colonial policy pursued by Britain was largely instrumental in destroying many of the Indian handicrafts and small industries whose products had a good market in Central Asia.

The objectively progressive consequences of the annexation of Central Asia for the future socio-historical development of the region cannot be extended to trace the positive effect of the Tsarist Russian rule in Central Asia over the the growth of its economic relations with India and other neighbouring countries. The cessation of internecine wars among the Khanates and the restoration of law and order and legal rights, etc., of foreign traders in the wake of the merger of Central Asia with Tsarist Russia did create favourable conditions for the development of more intimate economic relations with the neighbouring countries including India. But Tsarist Russia was a colonial power too and the colonial character of its policies in Central Asia, its colonial rivalry with Britain came in the way of the development of economic ties between the Central Asian and Indian people.

REFERENCES

1. *Travels in Central Asia by Meer Izzut-oolah in the years 1812-13*, Calcutta, 1872, p. 69.

2. *Ibid*. Burnes also obtained a draft for Rs. 5,000 from Indian merchants in Kabul to be paid at Bukhara. (See Alexander Burnes, *Travels Into Bokhara*, London, 1834, Vol. 1, p. 170).

3. Alexander Burnes, *op.cit.*, Vol. 2, p. 429.

4. *Ibid*.

5. *Ibid*. pp. 434-35

6. *Ibid*.

7. *Ibid*.

8. P.I. Nebolsin, *Ocherki torgovli Rossii so Srednei Azii—Zapiski Imp. Russkogo geograficheskogo obshchestva*, Kn. X, 1855, p. 313.

9. N. Khanykov, *Opisanie Bukharskogo Khanstva*, St. Petersburg, 1843, p. 175.

10. *Birdzhevie Vedomosti*, No. 106, 107, 1869, in *Turkistanskii Sbornik*, T. 26, 1869, pp. 1-47.

11. V.O. Klemm, "Sovremennoe Sostoyanie torgovili, v. Bukharaskom Khanstve", in *Sbornik geograficheskikh, topograficheskikh i statisticheskikh materialav po Azii*, vyp. 33, St. Petersburg, 1888, p. 51.

12. *Turkiston Viloytining Gazeti*, No. 23, 1889, cited by P.N. Raul'zade, *op.cit.*, p. 68.

13. *AVPR, F. Sredneaziatskii stol, 1860-1910, dok. 1341, Dokladnaya Zapiska V.O. Kemma o Sovremennom sostoyanii torgovii v Bukharskom Khanstve*, 1887, L. 5.

14. M.A. Babakhodzhaev, *Russko-Afghanskie torgovoekonomicheskie sviazi*, Tashkent, 1965, pp. 49-50.

15. V.F. Novitskii, *Iz Indii v Ferganu, Sbornik geograficheskikh, topograficheskikh i Statisticheskikh materialov po Azii*, Vyp. LXXVI, St. Petersburg, 1898, pp. 168-169.

16. D.N. Logofet, *Strana Bespraviya (Bukharaskoe Khanstvo i ego sovremennogo, Sostoyanie)*, St. Petersburg, 1909, p. 131.

17. A.F. Gubarevich-Radobylskii, *Znachenie Turkestana v torgovle Rossii s sopredel'nymi stranami Azii* in "Materialy dlya izucheniya Khlop-Kovodstva", Vyp. II, St. Petersburg, 1912, p. 131.

18. *Ts. GAUz. SSR*, F. I-473, d. 35, L. 28.

19. *Ts. GAUz. SSR*, F. I-1, op. 16, d. 984, L. 4, d. 719, L. 400.

20. D.P. Krasnovskii (ed.), *Vneshnaya Torgovlya Bukhary do voiny*, Tashkent, 1922, pp. 16-18.

21. *Obzor Zakaspiiskoi Oblasti za 1890-1896 gg.,* p. 462.

22. N.P. Kolomiitsev, *Chai, mirovaya torgovlia Chaem i vopros a Kazennoi Chainoi monopolii v Rossii,* Moscow, 1916, pp. 35, 105.

23. *Ts. GAUz. SSR,* F. I-46, op. 1, d. 361, L. 30b.

24. *Ibid.,* F. I-36, op. 1, d. 3691, L. 24.

25. G.L. Dmitriyev, *op. cit.,* pp. 120-21.

26. N.P. Kolomiitsev, *op. cit.,* p. 155.

27. A.F. Gubarevich-Radobylskii, *op. cit.,* p. 105.

28. *AVPR,* F. Konsul, v. Bombee, d. 110, L. 21.

29. *Turkestanskie Vedomosti,* No. 2, 1913.

30. A.F. Gubarevich-Radobylskii, *op. cit.,* p. 105.

31. See an article by M. Andreyeyev in *Turkestanskie Vedomosti* No. 89, 1908 under the title 'Nashi tovary na rynke Indii'.

32. *Turkestanskie Vedomasti,* No. 178, 1908.

33. *Turkestanskii Kurier,* No. 65, 1908 as reproduced in *Turkestanskii Sbornik,* T. 458, 1908, p. 149.

34. *Ibid.*

35. *Ts. GAUz. SSR,* F. I-36, op. 1, dd. 620, 782, 853, 1429, 1516, 1567, 1570, 1740-1744.

36. *Novoye Vremya,* No. 1367, 17(29) December 1879. According to *Moskovskie Vedomosti,* No. 170, 1889 Indian moneylenders extended credit not only to big Bukharans but also to Russian capitalists.

37. S. Aini, *op. cit.,* pp. 426-27.

38. V. Nalivkin and M. Nalivkina, *op.cit.,* p. 38.

39. *Novoye Vremya,* No. 1367, 1879.

40. A. Vamberi, *Puteshestvie po Srednei Azii,* St. Petersburg, 1865, p. 89.

41. V.V. Krestovskii, *V Gostiakh u Emira Bukharskogo Khanstvo,* St. Petersburg, 1887, p. 300.

42. See I.I. Geier, *Ves Russkii Turkestan.* Tashkent 1908.

43. *Ts. GAUz. SSR,* F. I-17, op. 1, d. 3933, F. I-22, op. 1, dd. 45, 2043.

44. G.L. Dmitriyev, *op. cit.,* p. 142.

45. P.N. Rasul'zade *op. cit.,* p. 116.

46. G.A. Arendarenko, *Dosugi v Turkestane 1874-1889,* St. Petersburg, 1889, pp. 349-50. Soviet scholars have taken a different view of the statement of G.A. Arendarenko regarding the earnings of the Indian

moneylenders. P.N. Rasul'zade appears to be endorsing it (*op. cit.*, pp. 117-119). But G.L. Dmitriyev finds it highly exaggerated. On the basis of archival records Dmitriyev has established that in Katta-kurgan alone for which the profession-wise break-up of Indian settlers is available Arendarenko's estimate is thrice the real figure of earnings derived on the basis of the actual number of Indians engaged in moneylending. Thus, only 55 out of 68 Indians living in Kattakurgan were moneylenders but Arendarenko treated them all as moneylenders. Dmitriyev finds Arendarenko's calculation at the rate of 120% interest also on the high side. He thinks that this rate prevailed only in abnormal years and the rate for normal years was 60% only (*op. cit.*, p. 28.)

47. *Ts. GAUz. SSR*, F. 1, op. 11, d. 39, L. 1-95.

48. *Ts. GVIA SSR*, F. 400, op. 263/916a, d. 326, L. 22.

49. G.A. Arendarenko, *op. cit.*, p. 361.

50. *Ts. GVIA SSR*, F. 400, op. 261/911, No. 111, L. 13-14.

51. I.I. Geier, *op. cit.*, p. 58.

52. *Ts. GAUz. SSR*, F. I-19, op. 1, d. 24868, L. 50. F. I-504, op. 1, d. 783, L. 75.

53. *Ibid.*, F. I-19, op. 1, d. 26793, L. 2.

54. G.L. Dmitriyev, *op. cit.*, p. 150. Also see G.L. Dmitriyev's article "Iz Istorii Indiiskikh Kolonii v Srednei Azii", in D.A. Ol'derogge, *Strany i Narody*, Kniga 2, Moscow 1972, pp. 238-39.

55. G.L. Dmitriyev, *op. cit.*, pp. 153-54.

56. E. Schuyler, *Turkistan, Notes of a Journey in Russian Turkistan, Khokand, Bukhara and Kuldja*, Vol. 2, London 1876, pp. 95-96.

57. The above details about Indian traders' role in the internal trade of Central Asia are taken from G.L. Dmitriyev's already cited paper in D.A. Ol'derogge (ed,) *Strany i Narody Vostoka*, p. 238.

5

From the History of Indian Colony in Central Asia*
(2nd half of the XIX Century-Beginning of the XX Century)

G.L. Dmitriyev

The earliest information about a large colony of Indians in Central Asia relates to the seventeenth Century and is to be found in local chronicles—the well-known among them being the historical work of Muhammad Yusuf Munshi entitled *Mukim-Khanskaya Istoriya* [12.84-85].

The control of commanding position in India's sea-routes by the Europeans helped the rise of caravan trade of Indians. This was seemingly the basic cause for the emergence of a large colony of Indian traders and moneylenders in the countries of Middle East in general and in Central Asia in particular.

The peculiarities of capitalism developing in India under the domination of British colonialism constricted the entrepreneurship of the emerging national bourgeoisie [14, 41, 55, 364, 374]; it promoted in the nineteenth and early twentieth centuries the emigration of the members of Indian business and usurious classes to the adjoining countries. This situation also created conditions which

---

* D.A. Oldderogge (Chief editor), *Strany i Narody Vostoka Indiya-Strana i Narod, kniga* II, Moskva, 1972, pp. 234-47.

helped the survival of Indian settlements in the neighbouring states of India.

Indian colonies continued to exist in Central Asia right up to the time of the Great October Socialist Revolution. The successors of these migrants were registered as permanent residents in the Census of population conducted in Central Asian Republics in 1926 [6, 9].

In the second half of the nineteenth and the beginning of the twentieth centuries there lived between 6 and 8 thousand Indians in Central Asia according to the calculation of the contemporaries [9, 333; 16, 60; 10, 181).[1]

The places in India from which these migrants came can easily be indentified on the basis of archival as well as some published sources. Foremost among these was Sindh (town of Shikarpur and its adjacent places); the region of Peshawar and the Punjab (towns of Lahore, Multan, Haripur, Ludhiana and Amritsar) came next. Among Indians there were also inhabitants of Kashmir, Delhi, Allahabad, Bombay and other places [13, 3; 27, 19; 3 f. И-1, op. 32, d. 280; 5, 24. XI. 1854, No. 20].

The enumeration of areas from where Indian emigrants to Central Asia came, enables us to conclude that the core belonged to West and North-Western India, *i.e.* the parts which are in the Republic of India and Pakistan.

Indian emigrants generally settled down in the Khanate of Bukhara and territories under its control. They lived in Bukhara, Gizhduvans, Vangazi, Vabkent, Karshi, Guzar, Yakkbag, Khatyrchi, Nurata, Ziyauddin, Shahrisabz, Karakul, and also in other vilayets [3, F. И-126, op. 1, d. 1132, 1133, 1134].

On the territory of Turkistan, the Indians lived in the towns and villages of Farghana and Samarkand regions and to a lesser extent in the Syr-Darya area. Indians were also found in Semirechiye and

---

1. The official data about the number of Indians was considerably reduced because the colonial bureaucracy of Russia did not register Indian Muslims residing in Central Asia.

Zakaspia regions [17]. It seems there were no Indian settlements in the Khanate of Khiva. However, Indian traders did come to Khiva on commercial missions for brief periods of 2 to 3 months.

Indians, as a rule, lived in Central Asia only temporarily. The maximum period of their stay in Turkistan and Bukhara was 10-15 years and thereafter the majority returned to their homeland. As a result of this specific peculiarity, there was a continuous renewal of the Indian settlements, maybe even annually because of the departure of some and the arrival of others. In majority of the cases the families of Indians stayed behind. Only occasionally wives and daughters accompanied Indians to Central Asia [15, Appendix 3].

There were both Hindus and Muslims among Indians in Central Asia. A considerable section among them consisted of Sikhs. Besides, there were some Parsis also.[2]

Many among the emigrant Indians belonged to the trading caste of Bhatia in Sindh. Along with them were Marwaris and members of the business and usurious caste, Bania. There also lived in Central Asia members of other trading castes—Lohanas of Sindh, Punjabi Khatris and Muslim Khojas and Bohras from Western India [3, F. И-d, op. 31, d. 677, ff. 9-10, 16; op. 32, d. 280, f. 473].

Indian migrants in Central Asia tried to live together. With this aim, they used the traditional hub of Central Asian economic life, the caravan-serai for residential purposes. In some places, where their numbers were large, the Indians occupied a number of caravan-serais (Tashkent, Bukhara and Samarkand) [3, F. И-126, op. 1, d8

---

2. Since neither the Russian nor the Bukharan statisticians counted Indian Muslims, it is extremely difficult to establish the proportion of each community among the Indians in Central Asia. On the basis of data preserved in archival documents, it can be hypothesized that Hindus and Sikhs formed the largest chunk of Indians living in Turkestan. Indian Muslims generally preferred to go to Bukhara. According to a calculation by an English agent Gulab Khan, at the beginning of 1880s there were 200 Muslims and 400 Hindus among Indians in Bukhara [5, 182, No. 587 Sec]

1133; 8a, 23, 26, 184]. Sometimes the houses of Indians were situated in one part of the city and were close to each other. Thus, they formed what came to be known as "Indian Section" (Stary Margelan, 80s of the nineteenth century) and "Hindu quarter" (Sardobin in the town of Nemangan at the beginning of the twentieth century) [3, F. И-19, op. 1, p. 10758, f. 53; d. 28889, f. 17].

The existence of compact Indian settlements in Central Asia was by no means accidental.

The feudal oppression prevailing in Central Asian Khanates till their union with Russia, compelled the Indians to think of collective defence which would be naturally more effective than the defence by an individual. On the other hand, many of them were traders and moneylenders, who made profits at the expense of the local native population. Hence, they were singled out by the local working population not on the basis of differences of nationality and religion but due to class contradictions. Knowing this, the Indians tried to stay together so as to collectively safeguard their class interests.

Amongst themselves the Indians selected as their leader a senior member, who was, according to Central Asian traditions, called Aksakal. These Aksakals were to be found in all places where there was a significant presence of the Indian community. After evaluating the archival documents we come to the following conclusions about the activities of the Indian Aksakals. He, when the need arose, contacted the Bukharan as well as Russian authorities on behalf of all the Indian residents of that place. He could either convey different demands of the local Indian population to the Bukharan or Russian authorities or carry on the orders of these bureaucrats, given in accordance with the prevailing law, to the Indian community [3, F.И1 op. 31, d. 848, f. 13; F.И126, op. 1, d. 96].

Consequently, the basic function of the Indian Aksakal was to remain in official contact with the Bukharan and the Russian authorities and to protect the interests of the Indian community as a whole. Naturally the Indian Aksakals could not perform all these functions on their own; they had to enjoy the trust of the majority of their countrymen or at least of the richer sections among them. It should be noted that the Indian Aksakals were not nominated by either the Bukharan or the Russian authorities; they were selected by the Indians themselves. The fact that mixed communities of Indians with an elected Elder existed, shows the presence of strong social ties amongst them and that intercourse between the 'pure' and 'not pure' existed in the activities of everyday life. The existence of these strong ties is confirmed by the interaction of the Indian community with the Bukharan and Russian officials.

For example, Bukharans and following them the Russian colonial officials, required the will of a deceased Indian in favour of his successor, to be testified by all the Indians residing in that place [3, F.И1, op. 29, d. 238, f. 2].

Besides this, the administration of Turkistan also required that all the Indians of the caravan-serai must testify to the 'trustworthiness' of their compatriot, when he was proceeding on a journey of Turkistan (3, F.И36, op.1, d.1477, ff.1, 3, 5, 9, etc.). In certain cases, the Russian officials allowed Indians a certain amount of autonomy in deciding civil cases; they did not have to go to the Court of Arbitration (3, F.И1, op. 22, d. 204). Sometimes the Indians were given the right to bail out their countrymen, accused of committing petty crimes [3, F.И36, op.-1, d.-621, ff. 209, 283].

In all probability, cases involving the entire Indian community residing at a particular place, were quite frequent and therefore the need arose for working out a steady term to designate them. In the documents in the office of Kushbegi of the Amir of Bukhara the term *hamai-hinduan* (the community of Hindus) was used for this (3, F.И126, op. 1, d. 93). Somewhat similar was the case with official Russian documents with the difference that the Turkistan administration could not coin a term to define this concept. In this connection the Russian officials used terms such as "Indian society", "community of fellow-countrymen", "colony", etc. [3, F.И1, op. 29, d. 238, f. 2; F.И17, op. 1, d. 1663, f. 1; F.И36, op. 1, d. 1287, f. 18].

This naturally does not mean that the Indians in Central Asia had anything of the type of a well-formulated and organised community. Each one among them earned his own living by his own efforts. They preserved amongst themselves their religio-caste distinctions. Under these conditions, the emergence of a community in the religious or secular sense embracing all Indians was an impossibility. In Central Asia could emerge and did spring up unions, which did not have full authority over all its affiliates. All this enables us to characterize the Indian community in Central Asia as a special type of association of fellow country-men.

In social composition the Indians were not homogenous. Among them the top position was occupied by traders and moneylenders. Along with them in the Indian settlements there were servants and members of low-castes. Of 136 Indians registered in Tashkent in 1875, 36 were servants of their countrymen and besides 5 were low-caste persons (3, F.И-17, d. 385, ff. 6-9). Similar picture can be seen in respect of Indian colonies in other places.

Social differences can be observed in the caste composition of the non-Muslim section of the Indian community. Along with members of business-cum-usurious castes, there also lived members belonging to the caste of the Kuli (3, F.И1, op. 31, op. 31, d. 677, f. 7, 9-10). The fact that individual Indians in Central Asia were engaged in agriculture is evident from the presence of the members of Indian castes among cotton growers (3, F.И5, op. 1, d. 2655, p. 13). Archival documents tell us of the presence of Indian jewellers, book-binders, weavers, bakers and Indian artisans in Central Asia [3, F.И36, op. 1, d. 3326, f.-10]. Finally, special attention should be paid to the data concerning the coming of Indian labourers in Turkistan at the beginning of the 20th Century [3, F.И1, op. 32, d. 213, f. 126]. Thus, proletarian elements were also present in the Indian colony.

Indian traders during the period under review brought traditional goods from India, tea, indigo, muslin, etc. The bulk import of these goods in Bukhara was in the hands of Muslim merchants of India. Its retail sale was carried on by the non-Muslim section of the Indian community in Turkistan. The norms of customs introduced after the union of Turkistan with Russia temporarily reduced the export trade of Indian merchants to Farghana, Samarkand and Syr-Darya territories during 1870s and 1880s. However, the Indians showed a continuing interest in the promotion of Indo-Central Asian trade and jointly with Bukharan traders took initiatives several times for its expansion [3, FИ1, op. 34, d. 524, f. 8]. Without waiting for a response from the side of the Tsarist authorities, the Indian traders along with their Persian and Bukharan counter-parts succeeded in increasing the import of Indian commodities to Central-Asia. In 1880s Indians refused to import their goods via Afghanistan and started exporting it to Central Asia via the cheap and safe route of Persia. After the opening of the Trans-Caspian Railway, they raised the issue of using the far more cheaper transit route—Bombay-Batumi-Kavkaz-Krasnovodsk [3, FИ1, op. 34, d. 714, f. 1-2]. The official permission to transport Indian goods by this route was received in 1894.

With the opening of the sea-route, Indian traders were partially able to re-establish their position in the markets of Turkistan, the trade in tea registered special growth. Between 1881 and 1892, not once Indian traders in Tashkent are referred to as dealers in tea. But in 1896 six Indian traders in Tashkent were engaged in the commerce of tea [3, F.И36, op. 1, d. 1962, f. 7; d. 3326, f. 10; d. 3691, f. 24]. In 1870s and 1880s Indian traders dealt in tea only on the territory of the Khanate of Bukhara. There were 8 to 10 wholesalers, hailing from Peshawar. After the opening of the sea-route, their numbers increased to 70 by the beginning of the twentieth century [3, F.И46, op. 1, d. 361, f. 2, 13]. Enjoying a monopoly in the tea markets of Bukhara, the Indians now penetrated gradually into the markets of Turkistan. In Samarkand, which became the biggest tea market in Turkistan, the Indians opened warehouses of tea. Of the ten such warehouses existing their in 1910, Indians owned three [3, F.И46, op. 1, d. 269, ff. 77-78].

By the end of the nineteenth and beginning of the twentieth century, the Indian traders had become more active in the sale of indigo and muslin in the markets of Turkistan, Khiva and Bukhara.

During this period they also exported from Central Asia, to Afghanistan and Kashgar and occasionally to India, commodities such as silk, Russian porcelain and manufactured goods (20).

The Indian traders actively participated in commerce between Turkistan and Central Asian Khanates. Their operations were specially massive towards the end of 1860s and the beginning of 1870s in the Khanate of Kokand. They brought to Tashkent from Kokand, cotton, hand-woven cotton textiles, Kashgar silk, wooleen and cotton material, robes, dyes, etc. They sent Russian iron, copper steel, cauldron, calico, sugar, etc., to Kokand (3, F.И-471, op. 1, d. 10, f. 10, 33, 44 and others.).

Right up to 1917, Indians used to sell Central Asian goods, produced by artisans and Russian factory-produced items in the bazaars of Turkistan. Sometimes Indian peddlers moved from village to village selling commodities (3, F.И-1, op. 32, 1.267, f. 441). The most important part of their activity consisted in the purchase of agrarian raw materials such as food grains, cotton, wool, fur, etc., (3, F.И-2, op. 2, d. 586, ff. 1, 2, 7, 10, 13).

After the union of Central Asia with Russia, the Indian traders began participating in commercial activities in the country-side. In course of time they established strong working relations with Central Russian firms, received from them regular supplies of commodities and participated in Nizhnegorod fairs [3, F.И-185, op. 1, d. 132, f. 100; F.И-1, op. 32, d. 247, f. 114].

An important section among Indian immigrants consisted of moneylenders who professed Hinduism or Sikhism. They became specially involved in moneylending in 1870s. In 1871, the Russian colonial administrators took the first steps towards restraining the moneylending activities of the Indians. The Military Governor of Zeravashan region wanted to prosecute Indian moneylenders on the basis of the prevailing laws (3, F.И-1, op. 20, d. 3677, f. 3). However, till 1877, effective measures were not taken. Only on 27 October 1877 the Governor General of Turkistan brought out a circular entitled "Ending the exploitation of the native population by Indian immigrants". It prohibited Indian moneylenders from taking possession of the landed property and agricultural lands of the defaulter [3, op. 27, d. 517, f. 5]. The introduction of this norm led to a reduction in the number of moneylenders among the Indian immigrants. It spurred Indians to participate more actively in the internal and external trade of Turkistan. Only in the Bukharan Khanate moneylending continued to have a prominent place in the activities of Indians right up to the beginning of the twentieth century.

Some of the Indian immigrants set up capitalistic enterprises. In 1887 Bai Bala Gulev received the right to mine gold. [3, F.И-1, op. 16, d. 208, f. 16). Individual Indians even in 1870s supplied raw materials to Russian factories: Paraman Lagurinov supplied raisins or *kishmish* to a wine-producing factory (3, F.И-46, op. 1, d. 1027, f. 245). The above-mentioned Bai supplied grapes (3, F.И-504, op. 1, d. 3109, f. 10). The tea-related enterprises belonging to Indian traders in Samarkand were also enterprises of capitalist type. In 1906 in the enterprise owned by Fazliahmedov of Peshawar 30 hired labourers were permanently employed. [3, F.И-46, op. 1, d. 136, ff. 213-214]. In 1909 in the enterprises of his compatriots, Shamsutdinov and Illahi Bakhsh, there were 23 and 10 hired labourers [3, F.И-46, op. 1, d. 269, ff. 178-179].

In 1896 Indian Bai Bala Gulev in association with A. Ya. Elifanov set up a cotton cleaning plant in the village Mashad in Namangan district. [3, F.И-504, op. 1, d. 783, f. 75]. Another migrant from India, Akub-Sheikh Nurkhanov from Peshawar set up a cotton-cleaning factory in Andijan [3, F.И-19, op. 1, d. 26793, f. 2].

The inhabitants of India, especially the non-Muslims could be sharply distinguished from the native population by their external appearance. Anthropological characteristics and dress distinguished the Indians. Their upper garment usually consisted of a square black cap, small and closely fitting dark gown painted with miniature figures, a cord belt, wide-trousers and leather shoes [22, 126].

The hair-style of the Indians was also distinct. In place of shaving the entire head as was the custom with the muslims, the Hindus shaved only the hair on the forehead. Their dark hairs were usually combed or allowed to fall almost up to the shoulders [11, 293].

During the period under review there are no indications in our sources that the Indians constructed buildings in Central Asia. Even in the Russian official documents the so-called Indian caravan-serai is described as a 'structure in native frame-work' [3, -18, op. 1, d. 13168, f. 5]. Consequently, the houses of Indian immigrants were indistinguishable from the houses of the natives.

The German traveller Albrecht, who entered into the Indian caravan-serai in Bukhara in 1890s informs us that the inner side of the wall enclosing the structure was whitened and against this background 'quaint' figures had been drawn in red colour. Again, according to information given by him, the walls of the dwelling houses inside the caravan-serai were decorated with motley gay coloured patterns [22, 123].

Thus, it can be presumed that inside their houses, the Indians tried to preserve their national colour designs.

The Indian migrants to Central Asia were prohibited from constructing temples and other religious buildings by the orders of the local Muslim rulers. Hence, they were forced to use the inner houses in the caravan-serai for religious purposes. In literature, descriptions of their religious rituals, performed inside the caravan-serais of Tashkent, Kokand and Bukhara have survived. According to these writings every worship house had an altar on which were placed a number of stone idols. In Kokand in the house of worship, besides idols there was a picture of Vishnu, kept in a special cupboard [26, 184; 24, 100; 25, 358].

The English traveller H. Lansdell, who visited Turkistan and Bukhara in 1880s writes that he saw a large number of books in the worship houses in Bukhara and Kokand. In Bukhara they were kept in a cupboard placed in the worship house, while in Kokand they were kept in an adjacent room. The most valuable book (probably a collection of religious hymns) was kept in the worship house in Kokand on the altar and was covered with a hanging (24, 100).

The collection of books kept in the worship houses shows that Indian migrants believing in this or that faith had in Central Asia some sort of a community library of religious books. This view is further strengthened by the fact that the Department of Collection of Jiziya in Bukhara noted on 12 Muharram 1307 A.H. (1889) that there were three holymen who looked after the library in the caravan-serai in Karshi. (The Persian words are *'se nafar pirzadah kitabkhana'* [3, F.И-126, op. 1, d. 93].

The Indian places of worship also contained icons. One of them was found in Tashkent. We do not know how it came from Banaras to Turkistan. According to description given, by the correspondent of *Prosveshcheniye,* a newspaper of Tashkent, it was a very old icon of goddess Kali'. It was painted on a board 'one *arshin* high and 3/4 *arshin* wide. It was fixed to a strong wooden frame with a strong chain' which probably held the icon to the wall and also held in place the thick glass which covered the face of the icon' [18]. [One arshin = 29 inches–trans].

The worship houses of Indian migrants were looked after by specialist-priests, called in Bukharan and Russian documents as "pirzadas". After their arrival on the Turkistan territory, these holymen from India requested from the concerned officials permission to stay. In their requests they mentioned that they had come here "to perform the duties of a spiritual person (priest) for serving the God, *i.e.,* for chanting religious hymns of the Hindus in the morning" [3, F.И-1, op. 32, d. 286, f. 330].

The statement of the Indian Tulasamal Sabraj given in 1907 is somewhat contradictory to the above. He informed the Russian authorities that he had come "with the aim to serve the house of worship of Hindu-sufis" (3, F.И-1, op. 32, d. 248, f. 179). If the authors of the document have correctly used the Muslim term for the Hindus, then they must be speaking of something akin to a lay-brother, in church, who generally performs the task of a muezin and looks after the cleanliness of the premises.

From what has been written, it follows that the duties of the person known by the name of 'pirzada' were completely heterogenous in the religious life of the Indians.

The following information contained in archival documents about an Indian *'pirzada'* deserves attention.

Most or almost all the Indians had left behind their families in India but these holymen were usually bachelors and they emphasized the fact that 'they were not married and that was the reason they were discharging the responsibility of a priest' [3, F.И-510, op. 1, d. 25, p. 15].

A *pirzada* staying in the city of old Margelan in 1880s, who had migrated from India "was very poor and lived exclusively on alms given to him by other Indians" [3, F.И-23, op. 1, d. 239, ff. 6-7]. Similar was the case with the Indian *pirzada* in Tashkent, Missar Amanomal "who was their (Indian's) holymen, looked after their house of worship and lived exclusively on charity of community members" [I.F. Glavny Arkhiv, P.-7, op. 43, 1882, d. 5, f. 330].

Finally the statement of Indian Baba Nachaldas is very interesting. He stated that "he wanted to live in Farghana region in place of his compatriot Ibkumal Hiraram, who was returning to the country" [3, F.И-1, op. 32, d. 261, f. 26].

The facts stated above lead to the conclusion that the Indian *'pirzada'* differed from his other countrymen in regard to his familial position. The *'pirzada'* was generally dependent on his 'parishoners', and amongst themselves had some sort of succession arrangement. This gives us enough ground to hold the view that amongst Indians in Central Asia members of the professional priestly class were present.

Indian migrants living in Turkistan and Bukhara continued to follow a distinctive life-style as is the characteristic of the adherents of Hinduism. Eye-witnesses reported: "Each Indian eats in his own cup and with his special spoon. He does not give it to anyone, even his own country-men. The utensil if touched by a member of another faith, is considered polluted, so is the fire if from it non-Indian takes a piece of coal" [21].

Within the Indian caravan-serai there existed shops "from where Indians received from Indians whatever they needed". This resulted in the presence of, within the Indian settlement, a group of service personnels. The Department for the Collection of Jaziya in Bukhara refers to bakers, cooks, sweet-meat makers, and even barbers among Indians [11, 293; 3, F.И-126, op. 1, d. 93].

In spite of leading such a distinctive life-style, the Indians have left some mark in the Central Asian literature. This is due to the fact that the Indians remained in daily contact and had permanent ties with the representatives of different sections of the native society.

There are a large number of references to the rituals which the Indians performed everyday throughout the year during their morning ablution. The place for the morning ablution was usually the canal passing through the Indian caravan-serai. If there was no canal, the Indians bathed by pouring water from head to foot. Sometimes, there were special structures in shape of bath-rooms which were meant specially for the performance of morning ablutions. Such a bathing place existed in the caravan-serai owned by an Indian Sufi Ramsu in Andijan in 1890s [3, F.И-511, op. 1, d. 65, f. 1].

Indians residing in Central Asia, held the traditional Hindu view and regarded cow as a sacred animal. Everyman, who visited Bukhara at the beginning of 1820s marked that the local Indians held cow to be sacred and bowed before it. [23, 76].

In accordance with the canons of Hinduism, non-Muslim Indians stuck to the traditional method of disposing the body of their deceased compatriots. Archival documents pertaining to the period under review mention this custom. Every time a compatriot died, the Indians informed the local Turkistan or Bukharan authorities. Administration then deputed persons from the police and the Justice Department to remain present when the body was cremated at a designated place [Bukharan term *Jari-i-makarpan*] [3, F.И-126, op. 1, d. 93].

It may be presumed that the representatives of local administration were present during the cremation of the corpses because the Central Asian Muslims considered the burning of the dead body as desecration of the remains of human body and could have obstructed the performance of this ritual [10a; 1894, No. 9].

The Central Asian population knew about at least two important Hindu festivals. One of them was in honour of Krishna. This has been referred to in the papers of the local Judge of Kokand. The Indians in Kokand celebrated it noisily and with much fan-fare on 25 February (9 March) 1879. It resulted in clashes with local population. The whole matter was referred to the local Judge [3, F.И-510, op. 1, d. 26, f. 1].

A great scholar of Turkistan, N. Lykoshin who visited the area wrote a detailed description of a similar festival, celebrated by the colony of Indians in Tashkent in February 1896. The celebration was marked by a party in which national Indian food was served; songs were sung in chorus accompanied by tambourine and clanging of bells. Finally, a procession was taken out [10a, 1896, No. 92].

The documents in the office of Chief Mirshab of the city of Bukhara contain a report by him of another Hindu festival. Unfortunately the report is not dated. But judged on the basis that the paper on which the report is written, is of Russian production, it can be confidently attributed to the period under study. The author of the document participated in the celebration held in the Indian caravan-serai "Karshi" at the invitation of some of its important residents. He calls it 'festival of lamps (*id chiragan*)'. In his words, the entire inner portion of the building was lighted by a large number of lamps [3, F.И-126, op. 1, d. 822]. This brief description shows that he was referring to the festival of Diwali held in the honour of goddess Lakshmi.

Indians residing in Tashkent celebrated this festival in the month of October. Their caravan-serai on this occasion was lighted by hundreds of kerosene lamps. As with the spring festival, this was also accompanied by lavish feasting. Musicians and singers sang songs 'of religious and poetic character'. As distinguished from the spring festival, during the autumn festival, the Indians refrained from consuming alcohol. And others "who ate meat of sheep on other occasion, on this day ate only vegetarian food' (10a, 1896, No. 92).

The special respect paid by the Indians to cow was well known and local people did take advantage of this. It is not accidental that the residents of Bukhara during the festival of the Hindus brought their cows to the Indian caravan-serai. The Indians daubed them with dry red colour and prayed to them. As a mark of gratitude to the owners of the cows, they fed the cows with seeds of cotton, something which most of the owners of the cows could hardly afford [22, 123].

The Bukharan Mirshab mentioned above, specially emphasized in his report that he was invited in accordance with the established custom (*bedastur har sal*). An invitation like this shows that a sizeable section of the native population of Bukhara was kept informed of important festivals celebrated by the Indian migrants. The same might be said of the residents of Tashkent. N. Lykoshin noted that during one of the festivals of the Hindus "the roof of the four-cornered serai (the Indian caravan-serai—G.D.) was full of curious native spectators; many of them even entered the court-yard and laughed with . . . the Hindus" [10a, 1896, No. 92].

Indian funeral customs were also well known in Central Asia. In 1890s crowds who gathered from the surrounding villages "sat through the entire ceremony" and witnessed it from close quarters [10a, 1894, No. 9]. Even the European population of Turkistan showed interest in the funeral customs of the Indians. From the description of N. Lykoshin given above, it appears that during one of the funeral ceremonies of Indians, many residents of the European part of Tashkent were present. It was also attended by the the Russian Head of the local administration along with his colleagues [10a, 1894, No. 9].

We have noted above some specific features of the life-style of the non-Muslim section of the Indian population which sharply distinguished them from the native population of Central Asia. On the basis of what has been already said it can be safely concluded that the Indians preserved the basic features which characterised their life-style in the mother country. Hence, it was possible for members of different social groups in Central Asia to get well acquainted with these. Many of these features, because of their specificity attracted the attention of a wide circle of local population, who thus got an opportunity of having a correct picture of the highly unique culture of their neighbouring country. Along with all this, it should be noted that in view of the extreme low literacy rate then prevailing, this live contact with the Indians was the only source for them to acquire knowledge and some conception of India.

The personal archives of migrant Indians which have come down to us contain a variety of documents in the Tajik language [2, Ms. Ind. IV, 22]. Along with receipts given by the loanees, we come across documents written by Indians themselves about their life-style. An example of this is the note written by Kripaldas addressed to his clients, "Kripaldas son of Jasu has left for Yangi Kurgan. Anyone who may have any work with him should contact him there" [2, Ms. Ind. IV, 22].

Some documents have survived which tell us about Indians, who were well-versed in the Uzbek language. One of them was Kabirshah Mustafin, a migrant from Kashmir, who lived with his family in the village of Bekabad of the Pskentski rural district of Tashkent in 1890s. Kripamal and Sukumal belonging to Shikarpur, who came to Tashkent in 1909 also knew the Uzbek language [3, F.И-1, op. 31, d. 586, f. 58]. Indians Sadumal Himanmalev, Hasa Hundayev, Gulyamal Himalmalev and Mushyamal Himanmalev knew the Uzbek language so well that they could testify in the Uzbek language in the court of the Judge at Skobeleo in 1913 [3, F.И-133, op. 1, d. 1389, f. 7].

All these facts show that Indians who lived especially in the rural areas and had to deal with the Uzbek population, learnt the language out of sheer practical necessity. There is enough evidence to presume that many Indians adequately knew the language of the local population because without its knowledge it was not possible to carry on their commercial and other activities.

After the union of Central Asia with Russia, the Indians had to perforce come in contact with Russian authorities, merchants and entrepreneurs for transacting their personal business. As a result many of them soon learnt the spoken Russian language. In 1870s in Tashkent there lived someone named Nukra Buta "who knew Russian language" [3, F.И-1, op. 16, d. 1001, f. 27].

However not all Indians mastered the Russian language. Probably because of this, there were some Indians who served their compatriots as interpreters. We have information about one of them—Pirdas Shavildasov, who lived in Tashkent in 1904 [3, F.И-1, op. 31, d. 282, f. 5].

Some evidence suggests that occasionally Indians tried to acquire a deeper knowledge of the Russian language. For example, an Indian Puran Singh, who lived in Samarkand in 1878, at the age of 32, joined the Russian School for adults. According to the evidence of the neighbours, he used to read Russian books throughout the night [3, F.И-5, op. 1, d. 2595, f. 6, 8].

In 1877-78, a 16-year Indian boy Mansok studied in the Primary Russian School in the city of Kattakurgan. The compulsory subjects taught in the school included, Russian language, Arithmetic, Catechism and religious history. However the teachers showed tolerance and did not compel the Indian boy to study religion, alien to him. Hence, he was examined only for his proficiency in Russian orthography and reading and in Arithmetic [3, F.И-47, op. 1, d. 82, f. 30]. According to contemporaries, the school where the Indian boy studied was the only school in Zeravshan territory where the children of the native population studied along with the Europeans and received not a formal but real knowledge of the Russian language [3, F.И-47, op. 1, d. 97, f. 3].

The fact that the Indian child studied in a Russian school along with Russian children is a shining example of the attitude of the Russian authorities towards the Indian immigrants. It is important to remember that in South Africa, the children of the so-called free Indians did not have the right to study in European schools [7, 189].

In course of time, there were cases when Indians lost touch with their motherland, acquired a family in Central Asia and settled down there permanently. The successors of these Indians did not always have a clear idea of their Indian language. Thus in the 1926 Census of Population of the Soviet Union, 37 Indians in Central Asia registered themselves as citizens of the USSR. Five of them gave Russian as their mother tongue and one-Uzbek [6, 9].

The study of Russian language by Indian migrants may be considered as the first link in the emergence of cultural contacts between India and Russia on the territory of Central Asia. As archival documents show, on this basis arose different forms of cultural exchanges between Indians and Russians on the territory of Turkistan region in Central Asia.

The above mentioned Puran Singh showed a definite inclination towards Russian literature. In 1890s, many Indians staying in Turkistan showed interest in finding out more about the cultural life of Russian Turkistan. An evidence of this is that Indians regularly attended Russian theatrical performances [3, F.И-1, op. 29, d. 1292, F. 1].

Many Indian migrants availed of the services of Russian Medical Institutions in the territory of Turkistan. In the Farghana region in 1887, 57 Indians turned to Russian doctors for medical help [15, 15].

The collection of Has Jas which contains his personal papers, has a prescription given to him by a Russian doctor. Has Jas spent considerable time in Central Asia [2, Ms. Ind., IV, 22]. This shows that the Indians used the services of medical clinics in Turkistan.

Indians living in the Khanate of Bukhara, where medical services were not available, often travelled to Tashkent and other cities of Russian Turkistan for consulting Russian doctors. Once in a while for this they even went to Moscow or Petersburg [3, F.И-1, op. 32, f. 270, f. 147; d. 280, ff. 175, 203, 263, 282].

Russian orientalists became interested in Indians, arriving in Central Asia after its union with Russia. P.I. Pashchino, the noted Russian orientalist in 1867 published an article "Stories of Kashmiris about their motherland". He had collected the material for this during his discussions with a Kashmiri in Tashkent. The article described the terrain, economy, demography and political structure of the kingdom and was probably the first research article on Kashmir in Russian language [8].

Individual Indians participated in academic expeditions sent to study Central Asia. One of these was Ramchandra Balaji, resident of Bithoor (in Central India). After the suppression of people's uprising in 1857 in India, Ramchandra, belonging to an aristocratic family, was taken by Englishmen to Europe, where he received his education. Having fled from the Englishmen, Ramchandra tried several times to return to his motherland. In 1878 Ramchandra arrived in Russia and spent some time in Central Asia [18]. His further attempts to return to his motherland seems to have failed and he was forced, according to English spies, to settle down in Constantinople [5, 1836, No. 18].

During his stay in Petersburg, Ramchandra became acquainted with several Russian scholars, including geographer, P.P. Somenov-Tyan-Shan, Indologist I.P. Minayev, Sanskritologist K.S. Kossovich, Orientalist V.V. Grigoriev and others. Their letters of recommendation preserved in the archives, show how highly they valued his intelligence and education [3, F.И-1, op. 1, d. 588, ff. 1, 6-7].

In the summer of 1887, Ramchandra with the Samar Academic Expedition extensively travelled in Central Asia. On the recommendation of the leader of the expedition, Ramchandra carried out reconnaissance of one of the ancient branches of the Oxus river—

Uzboya. According to many participants in the expedition, Ramchandra "fully justified the confidence and trust reposed in him" [3, FИ-40, op. 1, d. 17, R. 8].

By the end of 1890s the administration in Turkistan attempted to organise systematic training for Russian officers in oriental languages. In 1895 the issue for the teaching of Hindustani (the most popular language in North India) came up. For preparing teachers of this language the Russian orientalists enlisted wide ranging support from Indians residing in Central Asia.

In 1896 Lt. Vygornitskii was deputed to Bukhara to learn Hindustani by personally interacting with the Indians there as many of them were Hindustani-speaking. In the same year Junior Captain Gilferding was sent there on a similar mission. The later lived in Old Bukhara among Indians. One of the Indians agreed to teach him spoken Hindustani. He "taught his student some folk variations of the language, which could not be learnt from any text-book. He also taught him pronunciation of this language" [3, F.И-3, op. 2, d. 35, ff. 24, 62-63]. Gilferding had rich practical experience of spoken language during his frequent visits to the Indian caravan-serai and his talks with its inmates.

When courses in Hindustani language were started in 1897 in Askhabad and Tashkent, the Turkistan administration mounted a search for a capable teacher for teaching spoken Hindustani. For this preliminary inquiries were made among Indians by the local administrators even in the year 1895. A number of Indians were found in Samarkand and Bukhara, who expressed a desire to teach the language [3, F.И-3, op. 1, d. 359, f. 4, 6, 8].

Later in 1898, with the help of Russian Political Agent in Bukhara an Indian, Febdas son of Childas was found, who agreed to teach the students in Askhabad [3, F.И-3, op. 2, d. 35, f. 108].

During 1898-1899 practical teaching in Hindustani in Tashkent was conducted by the aforementioned Kashmiri, Kabirshah Mustafin. He enjoyed a deserving authority among Russian teachers because of his honest and conscientious approach to work. They all agreed that the success 'of the course was in no small measure due to him' [4, F. 1396, op. 2, d. 1532, ff. 9-10].

Afterwards the course in spoken Hindustani was taught by many other Indians. Some of them, according to the Course Director, acquired so much proficiency and skill in Russian language that they could teach the students without the help of European teachers [4, F. 1396, op. 2, d. 1662, f. 234].

The role of Indian teachers in conducting courses in Hindustani language was highly significant. The curriculum included regular conversation of the students with the teacher. The students had to answer their questions and translate their talk verbally into Russian. The Indians sat on the committee set up to examine the students. As a basic test, the student was required to act as an interpreter between the Examination Committee and his Indian teacher. He had to translate the questions and answer queries relating to life-style, religion, industry, etc., of India [4, F. 400, Aziatskay chast, op. 261/911, d. 520, ff. 9-11, 19].

Since several Indians went on holiday to their mother country, the Director of the Course asked them to purchase in India text-books and related literature and bring them to Turkistan [4, F. 1396, op. 2, d. 1589, pp. 181-182]. Later on, the teachers adapted these texts for the course, supplemented them with dictionaries and used them as reference material. Some of these were published in Tashkent by the lithographic method.

It should be noted that the courses in Hindustani conducted in Turkistan were the first systematic attempt to teach in Russia a living Indian language to a large number of people. Besides, many if not all, text-books and dictionaries, published in Russia towards the end of the nineteenth and beginning of the twentieth century either saw the light of the day in Tashkent or were prepared by people who were serving in Tashkent. All this enables us to view these courses as among the major events in the history of Russian indology.

To sum up

The Indian migrants to Central Asia in the second half of the nineteenth and beginning of the twentieth century formed part of the migration of Indians heading for the neighbouring countries. At the same time Indian migrants can be seen as comparatively small part of immigrants to Turkistan and Bukhara. But they were unique. The existence of the Indian colony was a significant stage in the history of economic and cultural relations between the people of India, Central Asia and Russia. In this region, the intercourse of Indians with the native as well as European population had its positive results. All this shows that the study of the history of Indian colony in the second half of the nineteenth and beginning of the twentieth century is interesting from the point of view of the history of relationship between the people of India and the Soviet Union.

LITERATURE CONSULTED

1. Arkhiv Vneshnei politiki Rossii
2. Leningradskoye otdeleniye INA AN SSR.
3. Tsentralnii Gosudarsvenyi Arkshiv Uzbekskii SSR.
4. Tsentralnyi Gosudarstvenyi Voenni Arkhiv SSSR
5. National Archives of India, Foreign Department.
6. Vsesoyuznay perepis naseleniya 1926, Vol. XV, Uzbekskaya SSR
7. Gandi, M.K., *Moya zhizn*, Moscow, 1959.
8. *Izvestiya Russkogo geograficheskoqo obshchestvo*, 1867, No. 6
8a. Kostenko, L., *Puteshestviye v Bukharu russkoi missii v 1870 g.* SPB, 1871,
9. Kostenko, L., *Turkestanskii kray. Opyt Voenno-statisticheskogo obozreniya Turkestanskogo Voennogo okruga.* Vol. 1, SPB, 1880.
10. Logofet, D.N., *Bukharskogo khanstogo pod ruskim protektoratom,* Vol. 1, SPB, 1911.
10a. Lykoshin, N.A., "Pismo iz tuzemnogo Tashkenta"—gaz. *Turkestanskiye Vedmosti*, 1896, No. 92.
11. Mayev, N., *Aziatskii Tashkent—Materialy dlya statistiki Turkestanskogo kraya*, Vyp. IV, SPB, 1876.

12. Munshi, *Mukimkshonskaya Istoriya*, Tashkent, 1956.

13. Nebolsin, P.I., *Ocherki torgovli Rossii s Srednei Aziyei,*—ZRGO, Book X, 1855.

14. *Novaya Istoriya Indii*, M., 1961.

15. *Obzor Ferganskoi oblasti za 1909* g., Skobelev z. 1911, Appendix.

16. Ostroumov, N.V., *Geografia Turkestanskogo kraya s kratkimi svedeniyami o khanstvakh Bukharskom, Khivinskom i Za zakaspiskoi oblasti*, Samarkand, 1891.

17. *Pervaya vseobshchaya perepis naseleniya Rossiiskoi imperii 1897g,* Vol. 82, 83, 85, 86, 87, 89, SPB., 1904-1905.

18. Petrov-Baturich, S.V., "Vstrecha s plemyanikom Nana-Saiba v Peterburge", *Russkii Vestnik*, 1879, No. 6.

19. *Prosveshcheniye*, Tashkent, 1918 (newspaper).

20. *Turkestanskii Vedmosti*, 1918 No. 2/44561 (newspaper).

21. Khorshkhin, A., "Samarkand", *Turkestanskiye Vedmosti*, 1872, No. 44.

22. Albrecht, M., *Russiche Centralasien*, Hamburg, 1896.

23. Eversman E., *Reise von Orenburg nach Buchara*, Berlin, 1882.

24. Lansdell, H., *Russian Central Asia,* London, 1885.

25. Lansdell, H., *Through Central Asia*, London, 1887.

26. Schuyler, D., *Turkistan, Notes of a Journey in Russian Turkistan, Khokand, Bukhara and Kuldja*, Vol. 1, London 1876.

27. Schwarz, *Turkistan—die Wiege der indogermanischen Volker*, Freiburg, 1900.

6

India and Central Asia:
Political Contacts from Colonial Period
to Aftermath of the Socialist Revolution*

Devendra Kaushik

Although Central Asia was incorporated into the Tsarist Russian Empire only in the later half of the nineteenth century (mid-sixties to mid-eighties to be precise), political contacts between India and Central Asia had already been influenced by the Anglo-Russian rivalry at the beginning of the century. The thinking of a whole generation of Indian historians has been somewhat in line with the basic tenet of British historiography that the aim of British diplomacy in the courts of Persia, Afghanistan and the Central Asian Khanates was to counteract the "Russian designs" in Central Asia and the proposed "Russian invasion" of India. Therefore, these Indian historians have tended to look at British policy solely as a defensive reaction to the "constant fear of invasion from the north-west" and the Russian designs in Asia.[1]

The real causes of rivalry between the two powers lay in strategical considerations and trade interests as well as in their desire to strengthen their control over the countries already conquered. The British colonialists feared that the approach of any foreign power to India's borders would inevitably lead to an outburst of popular anger against their rule. They were therefore eager to spread their

---

* Devendra Kaushik, *India and Central Asia in Modern Times,* New Delhi, 1985 pp. 81-117.

influence and, if possible, complete domination over the adjacent countries—Persia, Afghanistan, Sinkiang and Burma. Annexations on the part of both these powers were usually motivated by the need to obtain sources of raw materials and markets for their manufactured goods.

The nineteenth century witnessed an acute rivalry between Tsarist Russia and the British power in India over Central Asia. The British had set their covetous eyes on the Khanates of Central Asia—Bukhara, Kokand, and Khiva—and started collecting information about them even before they had extended the frontiers of their empire to the Indus and much earlier than the Russians had advanced towards them. Moorcroft and Trebeck of the East India Company can be called the pioneers of this policy of collecting intelligence about Central Asia in the second decade of the last century. They were ably assisted in this task by especially trained native agents like Meer Izzut-oolah.

Moorcraft records in his *Travels* how a certain Mulla Mohammed Amin shouted at him in Kunduz that he was engaged as a spy "preparatory to invasion of Turkestan",[2] and threatened to follow him to Bukhara. Moorcraft was saved through the efforts of one Mir Wazir Khan, a British agent, who had gone on his behalf to Bukhara and had found in the ruler of that state a disposition favourable to Moorcroft's visit to that city.[3]

Meer Izzut-oolah who travelled to Kokand, Samarkand and Bukhara and a number of other places in Central Asia in 1812-13 under instructions from Moorcroft has left a detailed description of the socio-economic conditions and of military strength of the Khanates. About Samarkand he noted that the "outer defences" of the city were "constructed of mud".[4] From the Kazi of Samarkand Izzut-oolah learnt about the seizure of Moscow by Napoleon and the great fire there compelling the French to evacuate the city.[5] Izzut-oolah also observed that the Bukharans had little capability to resist an invader as they had "no experience in real warfare" for a century. He further wrote: "They are generally armed with lances and what firearms they have are only matchlocks in the use of which they are not practised. With artillery they are well-provided, for in the fort of Bokhara alone there are number of guns lying about on the ground. They are, however, entirely unprovided with equipment, cattle, and ammunition required to bring their artillery into the field."[6] Izzut-oolah also mentioned about five or six serais for the merchants "such as that of Alum Khan Kao, generally used by Hindus and people of Shikarpur". Writing about the medical practitioners in Bukhara as "perfectly ignorant of the healing art", he noted that most of them came from Peshawar and Kabul and had "lucrative practice".[7] Among the articles exported to Bukhara from Peshawar, Kabul and Shikarpur, Meer Izzut-oolah mentioned woollen cloth turbans, white cotton cloth, chintz, molasses, sugar, turmeric, pepper and books of Muslim theology and law.[8]

At about the same time when Meer Izzut-oolah was traversing the inhospitable deserts of Central Asia at the behest of his colonial masters, Russian emissaries, Rafailov, a Jew, Shargilov, an Armenian and Madatov, a Georgian were commissioned to undertake a journey to Kashmir. However, only Rafailov and Shargilov could go farther than Semiplatinsk. Rafailov brought back to Semiplatinsk some beautiful Kashmiri shawls. He was awarded a gold medal by Tsar Alexander I. About the Kashmiris Rafailov wrote: "The people of the whole country are healthy, beautiful and cunning and practical but extremely hospitable".[9] He also lavished praises on the "beautiful green and fertile land" of Kashmir "abounding in horticulture".[10] Rafailov again passed through Kashmir on his way to Tibet in 1813 to be followed soon by the Georgian Madatov who reached Kashmir through Kashgar and met the local ruler who presented him shawls and expressed his desire to establish trade contacts with Russia.[11] In 1820, Rafailov and Dr. Eversman were sent on a mission to Kashmir and further to Maharaja Ranjit Singh of Punjab. But none of them could reach Lahore. While Rafailov died not far off from Kashmir, Eversman could not go beyond Bukhara due to unsettled conditions then prevailing in the region.

According to Moorcroft who visited Leh at about the same time, Rafailov who died near the Karakoram Pass was carrying a letter for Maharaja Ranjit Singh of Lahore. This undelivered letter was recovered by Moorcroft who sent it to the Government of India in 1821. The letter written by the Foreign Minister of Russia, Count Nesselrode, expressed the Russian Emperor's desire to open "the gates of friendly intercourse" and to "clear the road of traffic between the merchants of Russia and the Punjab from all impediments."[12] The well-known Russian Orientalist V. Bartold wrote that Rafailov had been sent to Kashmir from Semiplatinsk to implement a project for breeding Kashmiri goats in Siberia.[13]

Filip Yefremov was perhaps the first Russian to meet the Kashmir ruler during his tour of Kashmir in 1779-80. He was taken prisoner by the Kirghiz tribes who sold him as a slave to the Bukharans from whose captivity he managed to escape-reaching Kashmir via Kokand, Kashgar, Yarkand and Ladakh. Kashmir was then ruled by the Afghans. From Kashmir, Yefremov reached Calcutta from where he sailed to London and thence to St. Petersburg. In 1782 he was honoured by the Russian Empress. Somewhat later in 1795 a Georgian merchant Danibegov travelled to Pondicherry, Madras and Calcutta by sea from Turkey returning to Russia overland via Kashmir, Ladakh and Yarkand. Danibegov took interest in shawl production in Kashmir.

Between 1873 and 1875 Pashino, a member of Russian Foreign Service, made several unsuccessful attempts to meet the Maharaja of Kashmir and visit his kingdom. Earlier in 1869-70 he had travelled to Gilgit, Skardu and Leh but abandoned his mission to convey a message to the ruler of Kashmir upon learning about the presence of the Lt. Governor of Punjab in Kashmir. In 1873 he reached Jammu and met Dewan Jwala Sahai who directed him to go to Lahore and obtain permission from the British. The third Russian attempt to establish diplomatic contact with Kashmir also failed when Pashino was prevented from crossing the Punjab borders towards Kashmir in 1875.

Lord William Bentinck favoured the despatch of a British agent to Kabul and suggested that the (British agent) should be authorized by means of natives "to extend his inquiries to Bukhara and towards the Oxus and Russia". The British authorities in India even favoured the stationing of an agent at Tbilisi (Georgia).[14] Lt. Conolly of the 6th

Regiment Light Cavalry travelled to India from Astrabad on the Caspian through the territory of the Turkoman tribes and Herat and Kandhar to Shikarpur in Sindh in 1830. He also tried to go to Khiva but was prevented by a Turkoman tribe on the way. Lt. Conolly's *Memoirs* contain interesting information about the countries situated between the Caspian and the Indus with reference to both commercial and political spheres.[15] Conolly estimated the value of Bukhara's trade with Russia at about eight million roubles. During Lord William Bentick's tenure as Governor-General, Travelyan and Captain Pottinger were also deputed to make suggestions regarding improvement in British trade with Central Asia. All these three officers recommended that the Amir of Sindh be persuaded to reduce transit duties. Opening of the navigation of Indus was also suggested by them. They believed that given access to the Central Asian markets the British goods could in a few years completely drive out the Russian goods. Conolly pleaded for "identity of interest between the Afghans and Turkomans and the Honourable Company's Government which might possibly at some future period be turned to an important political account."[16] The Secret Committee, it may be recalled, "authorised the Government to depute an envoy even to Bukhara should they consider such a measure likely to promote the objects in view."[17]

In the early 1830s an expedition to Bukhara was led by a British intelligence officer, Lt. Alexander Burnes who collected military and socio-political information needed by the British for their future expansion in Central Asia. Mohan Lal, a Kashmiri Pandit accompanied him in his mission. Burnes' other companion was a Muslim surveyor Mahommed Ali who travelled in the garb of a pilgrim proceeding to Mecca. As it was not safe for Burnes to maintain a record of his travels, Mohan Lal who knew Persian very well "kept a minute journal of events" at his request.[18] During his stay in Bukhara Burnes was "most intimate" with his landlord, an Uzbek merchant, named Mukhsoom who paid him "a daily visit and generally brought some of his friends along with him". About him Burnes writes: "He was most communicative and gave us much useful information. As our intimacy increased, I interrogated him closely on the revenues and resources of Bokhara, on its extent and power, and once opened a small map of the country in his presence. He replied to all my enquiries; and then, begging I would shut up the map, beseeched me never again to produce such a paper in Bokhara since there were innumerable spies. . . . He still continued his visits and his information with the same freedom as before."[19]

Burnes' account is, however, highly informative so far as the social profile of Bukhara is concerned. About its bazaars he wrote: "Sufficient to say, that almost every thing may be purchased in the Registan: the jewellery and cutlery of Europe, (coarse enough however), the tea of China, the sugar of India, the spices of Manila, etc."[20] In Burnes' estimate there were about 300 Hindus living in a caravan-serai of their own in Bukhara, majority of whom came from Shikarpur. He testified to an increase in their number during the last few years[21] and to their prosperous business. Burnes also recorded his meeting with a deserter from the Indian Army from Bombay, a Hindu, who had "set out on a pilgrimage to all the shrines of the Hindu World and was then proceeding to the fire temples on the shores of the Caspian."[22] Among his friends in Bukhara Burnes makes a special reference to a Kashmiri merchant Ahmedjooee who wished him to help him in the preparation of cochineal which though found in Bukhara was not prepared there.[23] Burnes' observation about the Bukharan Uzbeks that they differed little in their features from the Persian-speaking people and that they did not possess the harsh features of the Uzbeks from Orguny[24] (the ancient Khwarezm), is of considerable interest for an ethnographic study of the Uzbek people.

That the Burnes mission was mainly aimed at obtaining political and military intelligence is apparent from the account given by Mohan Lal in his *Travels*. The Kashmiri companion of Burnes expressed the opinion that the climate was ripe for establishing "commercial or political" relations by the British with Bukhara and emphasized that "no time ought to be lost" in this, for "no power is likely to anticipate our (the British) intentions at present."[25] Mohan Lal collected detailed intelligence about the military strength of Bukhara.[26]

In 1838 Herat became a centre for British intelligence and surveillance activities in Central Asia, which were directed by Major

D'Arcy Todd. Col. Stoddart was sent to Bukhara from the British Consulate in Teheran. Other agents were despatched from Herat to Khiva and Kokand. In 1839 Major Todd sent to Khiva a certain Mulla Hussain who presented a rifle to the Khan. Soon Capt. James Abbott followed him there. He fell into Russian hands on 1 May 1840 while engaged in reconnoitring roads and fortresses near Novo-Alexandrovsk. When arrested he produced a forged document to show that he was a representative of the Khan. He was sent to London from Orenburg via St. Petersburg.

To affirm that the British waged the First Afghan war in the 1830s for the defence and security of their Indian possessions threatened by the southward expansion of Russia is to repeat the worn out alibi put forth by the British colonialists to justify their 'forward policy'. The First Afghan War occurred at a time when the expanding empire of Tsarist Russia was yet far from the frontiers of India and when the British too had not annexed Punjab and Sindh. This aggressive war was imposed upon a not unfriendly Afghanistan at a time when the siege of Herat by Persia had been abandoned and the Russian agent Vitkovitch had been recalled and repudiated. The Russian Foreign Secretary Count Nesselrode admitted to the British Ambassador in St. Petersburg that Count Simonich had exceeded his instructions and he also gave assurance on behalf of the Russian Government not to have any political relations with Afghanistan.

According to Rawlinson, James Abbott who was sent to Khiva by Major Todd had proposed after the fashion of the days of Malcolm and Elphinstone that Russians should be permanently excluded from the areas and "a defensive-offensive alliance was suggested with England, as a reward for this breaking with the common enemy". He, however, writes that Abbott in doing so exceeded his instructions which only related to the liberation of Russian slaves.[27] Vambery attributes to the British the plan of forming "an offensive-defensive alliance" against Russia with the three Khanates.[28] But he finds fault with the choice of Stoddart and Conolly who proved unfit to attain this object.

The British, Rawlinson observes, were "preparing to occupy Syghan, on the northern slope of the Hindukush and a further advance on Bukhara" in the late 1830s,[29] which could not materialize because of the Afghan resistance. During the Crimean War the British had planned to induct a strong force into Central Asia through Georgia. But as they "could never reckon on French cooperation", the plan had to be given up.[30]

In the 1840s the British intensified their operation of dumping textile goods in Bukhara at lower than cost price from both sides, *i.e.,* from India and Black Sea. The Report of the Department of Foreign Trade confirmed a fall in Russian textile export to Bukhara during 1845-47.[31] In 1852, Klycharyov complained about the fall in prices of Russian textiles on account of extraordinary export of British goods to all Central Asian Khanates in that year.[32]

For some time, the British approach to Central Asia remained on a low key on account of the difficulties created by the 1857 uprising in India. But in the early sixties they again intensified their intelligence activities in Central Asia under the direction of Col. Walker, Superintendent of the Great Trignometrical Survey. Col. Walker was assisted in this task by a group specially trained native agents, prominent among whom were Pandit Munphool, Faiz Mohd., Bhai Diwan Singh and Ghulam Rabbani. According to a veteran Indian surveyor, the years 1865 to 1885 were "the most fruitful for Indian explorers who, trained by the Great Trignometrical Survey of Dehradun, explored the uplands of Tibet, Mongolia and Central Asia".[33]

In 1863, Col. Walker and Capt. Montgomerie set about to train Indian explorers who might explore the uplands of Central Asia. Already in the opening decades of the nineteenth century British officers of the East India Company, men such as Moorcroft, Trebeck and Burnes, had trekked through the difficult and rugged mountainous terrain in the north-west frontier region and the inhospitable desert beyond and had trained a host of Indian travellers like Izzut-oolah, Fazil Khan and Mohan Lal in the art of counting paces and keeping accurate notes. Col. Walker taught them at Dehradun to take latitudes by sextant and directions by compass and determine the altitude by observing a thermometer in boiling water.

Yet all this was not motivated by a simple desire to locate Yarkand more accurately on the map and remove the uncertainty regarding the position of Lhasa in longitude or, as Col. R.H. Phillimore writes in his foreword to Indra Singh Rawat's book[33], "to satisfy the craze for knowledge of the unknown." It is not just a mere coincidence that the two decades of extensive explorations in the north-west region by the Great Trignometrical Survey were also the years of incorporation of Central Asia into the Tsarist Russian Empire. The translation of the diary of one such 'explorer' Ghulam Rabbani who visited Tashkent soon after the city was annexed by Tsarist Russia is preserved in the State Archives of Punjab at Patiala. Rabbani hardly conceals that the object of his mission was to gather military and political intelligence about Central Asia. Leaving Peshawar on 10 September 1865, Rabbani returned home in early 1867. During this period he visited Bukhara, Kokand, Khojent, Samarkand and Tashkent. After staying in Bukhara for two months and eight days Rabbani proceeded from there to Kokand in February 1866, staying there for one month. At Bukhara he made "acquaintance with members of the Bukhara Court" and sent a detailed report on this.[34] He gave an exhaustive description of surrounding areas, the circumference of the town of Bukhara, width of its walls with 12 gates, which in his opinion were not "capable of defence". He also wrote that "the army was indisciplined" and had 200 guns which were quite useless. Information about the military equipment and defence potential of Chiragchi, Shahr-i-Subz (in Bukhara) and the Russian fortifications near Jizzak was also sent by him.[35] With the help of Mulla Iwaz Muhammad, Mirza Baba Kitabdar and the news writer Muhammed Niaz, he gained an audience with Khan Khudayar Khan of Kokand. Ghulam Rabbani did three trips to Tashkent from Kokand to make a meticulous study of the fortifications, reservoirs, etc. He even mentioned such minute details as colour of the water in the rivers and the nature of the rocks and minerals. Eagerly exploiting the opportunity created by a panic prevailing among merchants on account of the Russian seizure of Tashkent, Rabbani offered to approach the Russian General Chernyayev for ensuring the safety of their lives and property. This voluntary offer of 'humanitarian' service to the Kokand merchants was in reality a cloak like the 'purchase of horses' and 'liberation of Russian slaves' on previous occasions. Ghulam Rabbani candidly recorded in his diary: "No one would risk his life by undertaking this journey (to Tashkent), but the writer who had an object in view volunteered to do this".[36] The object becomes apparent when we find him following General Chernyayev to the Chirchick river in the suburbs of Tashkent, keeping a watch on his movements. On his return to India Rubbani was accompanied by a *Vakil* of the Bukhara court. At Balkh they met Faiz Mohammed (another British agent 'explorer') and left for Badakhshan on urgent summons by his colleague, Bhai Diwan Singh, leaving the Bukhara emissary alone in his journey to Kabul where he joined them a little later.

Nazir Ibrahim Khan's account of his visit to Bukhara in 1869-70[37] preserved in the National Archives of India in New Delhi is another documentary evidence throwing light on the real character of the British sponsored travels to Central Asia. The writer records: "Having been deputed to Bukhara for the purpose of collecting information regarding the state of the country, the progress of the Russians, etc. etc., I set out from Peshawar on the 30th August 1869 and arrived at Kabul on the 9th September."[38] Nazir Ibrahim Khan reached Bukhara on 17 October 1869 and stayed there in the serai of Badrud-din where Indian merchants from Peshawar used to reside. He gave himself out as an agent of one Abdul Hamid of Peshawar and was obliged to leave the city for Samarkand on 14 November when the news of the demise of Said Abdul Hamid reached Bukhara. At Samarkand Nazir Ibrahim Khan stayed with one Abdul Majid, a Peshawari merchant. Here he collected detailed information about the disposition and strength of the Russian troops, which he attached to the account of his visit as an appendix.

Nazir Ibrahim Khan gives many interesting details about the Russian administration of Samarkand. He writes about a Russian officer Abramof who gave his quick judgement on petitions presented to him in the fort. "The officer is well versed in Persian and Turkic language", writes Ibrahim Khan. At Samarkand he also met one Sayyid Khan, a deserter from the 21st King's Native Infantry in India through whose assistance he was able to visit the fort. "The fort at Samarkand", he writes, "contains three infantry and two cavalry regiments and 24 guns." Sayyid Khan, the deserter from the British Indian Army, held the rank of a subedar in the Russian Army.

The picture of Russian rule in Central Asia drawn by Nazir Ibrahim Khan is quite favourable. "The landholders and people of Samarkand", he writes, "generally are at present satisfied with the Russian rule." The free mixing-up of the Russians with the natives of Turkistan must have come as a big surprise to an Indian subject of the British dominion hardly used to such a sight in his home country and he records at some length the free and uninhibited social intercourse between the European Russians and the Asian Turkistanis. He writes: "The Russians mix freely with the people, and the different classes associate together without difficulty. They often eat together, go to *hamams* (public baths) together and places of amusements together, etc. They converse with each other in the Turkic language. The respectable men of the city such as Qazis, Kotwals and merchants often entertain the Russian officers and in return dine with them."[39]

Ibrahim Khan's account also mentions the great interest taken by the Russians in the cultural heritage of Central Asia. He writes about a Russian Officer at Samarkand, who was engaged in "copying extracts from different Arabic, Persian and *Kafir* (infidel) authors, and transcribing passages from the Koran and historical and poetical books, etc." He records that this Russian officer "also copied the inscription on the tomb of the Amir Timur" and refers to the rumour that the Russians intended to restore and repair this tomb.[40] Ibrahim Khan also narrates his meeting with one Feroz Shah who called himself the son of the late Mughal Emperor of Delhi. Feroz Shah accompanied the army of the Amir of Bukhara in his last battle against the Russians at Jizzak. The Amir who was displeased with him on account of his vanity and arrogance stopped his allowance. After wandering about for some time Feroz Shah reached Samarkand and produced two or three Punjabi goldsmiths to testify to his identity. But when an inquiry was instituted, one Zahir Khan, formerly a clerk in the Peshawar Collectorate and another Indian named Reza Ali swore on the Koran that he was not Feroz Shah, the Prince. Thereupon the Governor of Samarkand directed him to leave the city.[41]

The travelogue of Ibrahim Khan contains valuable information about the state of India's trade with Central Asia. He refers to the preference of the people of Bukhara for Indian tea, long cloth and chintz to the same articles from Russia owing to their superior quality, but adds that they are obliged to purchase the Russian articles in consequence of their abundance and cheapness in the market. He attributes the high prices of Indian goods to the expense and risks involved in transit through Afghanistan. Ibrahim Khan ascribes the great demand for shawls and pashmina from Kashmir and Amritsar to their use by the Bukharan authorities for presentation as *Khilats* and gifts for Russian authorities.[42] He writes "Most of the Amritsar pashmina is bought up for the King for robes of honour and presents to Russian envoys, etc."[43]

Nazir Ibrahim Khan's account concludes with the narration of conversations among the merchants of Kabul and Peshawar in Samarkand about the forthcoming Peshawar trade fair. Some copies of a printed notice of the Peshawar fair had been received in Samarkand from Bukhara. The merchants of Bukhara intended to see how the Peshawar fair went on that year before venturing their goods in view of the previous year's slack sales at that fair.

Thus, Nazir Ibrahim Khan's document on his travels in Central Asia is really a rich mine of information about the manifold contacts between the peoples of India and Central Asia in the later half of the nineteenth century. Though he was sent to serve the aggressive designs of British imperialism in Central Asia, the record left behind by him serves a noble cause by refreshing the memories of close intercourse forged in the past by the people of India and Central Asia notwithstanding the barriers which both the British and Tsarist Russian colonialists sought to raise in their way.

The Russian advance against the Khanates of Kokand and Bukhara in the mid-sixties of nineteenth century brought the problem of gathering intelligence about these remote regions to the fore. The Punjab government proposed, on 7 June 1866 to the Foreign Department of the Government of India, to have agents accredited to one or more of the states of Central Asia "to keep us informed of the progress of events."[44] But the Governor General in Council decided against such a move and informed the Punjab government on 27 June 1866: "But whilst the Governor General in Council admits it to be very desirable that such information as may be procurable should be obtained, His Excellency in Council does not consider it expedient to have agents in the different states in Central Asia. No agents could be established permanently from whom the British government might expect to secure reliable information. Unless they took to intrigue, and, by reporting only what was agreeable to the Durbar, played into the hands of the chief to whom they might have been accredited such agents would not be allowed to remain in the country. The Government of India could not effectively protect them". The Governor General in Council concluded that "there is no other practicable mode of obtaining information than to act as we are now doing, that is, to procure news as we best can through native merchants and travellers and at suitable intervals to depute agents carefully and specially selected for the purpose of gaining intelligence".[45]

The Governor General, John Lawrence considered it "desirable to urge on the Home Government the necessity of endeavouring to come to terms with Russia in regard to Central Asian Affairs". Two members of his Council, Sir W. Mansfield and Noble Taylor suggested an "interchange of Consuls at Tashkund and Lahore" as the "best way of bringing about a proper understanding between the two nations in regard to Central Asian affairs".[46] R. Temple, another member of the Council, however, disagreed to this suggestion on the ground that the political effect of the presence of a Russian Consul at Lahore would be quite far-reaching as "among the other things it would be regarded by the Punjabees as a proof of the progress of Russian influence". He concluded: "Lahore is a place of infinitely greater importance than Tashkund. And I would not be for yielding the point unless we could obtain some really valuable concessions from Russia in respect to Central Asia".[47]

Thus, the British authorities in India continued to keep themselves informed of events taking place in Central Asia through native merchants and agents sent there from time to time. These agents were despatched by "F.B." who directed his intelligence-gathering operation in Central Asia for the Punjab Government. Thus, the Punjab Government forwarded to the Secretary of the Foreign Department of the Government of India in July 1876, the English translation of a newsletter received from "F.B.", confidential Agent to the Punjab Government, regarding the Russians in Kokand.[48] It informed about the arrival in Lahore (in the middle of April 1876) following the conquest of Kokand by the Russians) of Ishan Muhammad Meman, the spirital guide of the Muslims in that territory, accompanied by Nazar Kul, the former Governor of Namagan and eighty disciples and dependents on his way to Mecca. In Kabul Ishan met the Afghan Amir whom he tried to "alert against the tricks of the Russians" by giving him an "example of their encroachment on Kokand". The Afghan Amir was reported to have replied that "the Kokandis had only fear from the Russians while he has it from them as well as from the British".[49] That it was the practice of the Government of India to recruit persons knowledgeable about Central Asia for collecting intelligence is evident from the official records of the period preserved in the National Archives of India. We have the application dated 22 November 1867, of one Hukeem Mahomed Saeed Khan a native of Persia then residing in Lucknow, seeking employment as an agent. Hukeem who began his application thus: "As it is the wish of Government to have intelligence of the affairs of such places as Balkh and Bokhara, as well as to be supplied with information respecting the Russian troops. . . .",[50] offered his services stating that he had "full knowledge of the manners of the people of several towns of Afghanistan, Persia and Turkistan, such as Balkh and the neighbouring places of Bokhara".[51] He also claimed acquaintance with the nobility of the areas.

The British were successfully operating an elaborate network of intelligence in Central Asia in the early 1880s through their agent Gulab Khan living in Kattakurgan. Gulab Khan went to Central Asia accompanied by his wife and opened a druggist's shop in Kattakurgan. He enlisted the support of two Indian Muslim ex-Army men—Ghulam Mohiuddin of Rawalpindi district and his cousin Said Khan (son of his father's sister). Ghulam Mohiuddin was a Naib Ressaldar in the 13th Bengal Cavalry, who had joined the Army in 1857, the year of the mutiny, and remained stationed at Delhi for four years. He was made to resign from the army because of his indebtedness. Said Khan had deserted the British Indian Army after misappropriating official money. He served as drill instructor in Kabul and then left to join the Bukharan army as a Captain of the infantry in which capacity he worked for two years. He crossed over to the side of the Russians with sixty other natives of India and became an Assistant Commissioner or *Pomoshnik.*[52] Through Said Khan's contacts, Gulab Khan obtained important information from the interpreter of the Governor of Samarkand and the Kotwal. Gulab Khan also befriended a Jew named Reuben whose two cousins worked as interpreters to the Russian Governors at Samarkand and Tashkent.

During 1881-82 Gulab Khan sent valuable information to Lahore about the correspondence of the Maharaja of Kashmir and the contacts of the Kuka Sikhs with the Russian authorities in Tashkent and Samarkand through his couriers Ghulam Mohiuddin, Sharaf Din (both Indians) and Mullah Ikram, a Tadjik from Kattakurgan.[53] It was on the basis of information provided by Gulab Khan that Gurcharan Singh, the Kuka emissary to the Russians was arrested. Gulab Khan and his agents were given handsome monetary rewards by the British, and the Governor-General in Council condoned Said Khan's offence of embezzlement of official money while in service with the British Indian Army.

Gulab Khan in his letter of 26 January 1882 from Kattakurgan, sent through Mullah Ikram, gave detailed information about the correspondence of the Kashmir ruler and the Kukas with the Russians. He had obtained this information through Said Khan. According to him Karam Prakash Udasi, employee of the Kashmir ruler, was sent to Tashkent by Sardar Attar Singh, Head of the Jammu Secret Intelligence Department, with a letter from the Maharaja. The purport of the letter was to this effect: "We obey the English Government because Russia is far off. When you come in this direction we will serve you. All the notables throughout Hindustan are disaffected to the English".[54] A *Khillat* was presented to the emissary. Earlier in 1872 one Sher Singh Brahman of Rajaori who was *Hakim* of Supar in the Baramulla Circle was sent by the Maharaja of Kashmir along with Sham Das Suri, a Khatri of Baisun to General Kaufman at Tashkent. The Kashmiri emissaries told General Kaufman that their ruler desired to be on friendly terms with the Russians. Sher Singh returned home together with Karam Prakash leaving behind Sham Das Suri. According to Gulab Khan one Eshar Das Brahman of Phagwara in Kapurthala State accompanied Karam Prakash to Jammu and then returned to report his safe arrival there. Eshar Das who was living in Kattakurgan was believed to be planning to go back home during that year.

Gulab Khan in his same letter recalled that he had reported in 1880 about Abdul Wahab of Yusufzai who was sent to Kashmir as a Russian emissary. Abdul Wahab returned to Tashkent with Jiwan Mal Dogra and brought a letter from the Maharaja. The letter from the Russians had said: "We are sending Abdul Rahman Khan to Kabul. Raise a disturbance when he engages the English". To this the Kashmir ruler's reply sent through Jiwan Mal Dogra ran as follows: "You are preparing for war with China. When you have conquered them I will do whatever you tell me. You have not even crossed your border. How then can I raise a disturbance till you advance?"

The letter from Gulab Khan also mentioned that after Karam Prakash's mission Sardar Attar Singh sent another emissary named Ganga Ram Dogra, a Brahman of Dhanisal in the Raisi district of the Jammu territory with some message of the Maharaja. Ganga Ram remained at Samarkand for four years and petitioned General Abramov to be allowed to learn Russian language in a Russian School. Ganga Ram acquired proficiency in Russian and became a *Tahsildar* on his return to Jammu. According to Gulab Khan's information he was then staying at Dhanisal. Ganga Ram was described by him as having a pock-marked face with one eye almost closed.

Gulab Khan wrote about yet another Kashmir emissary-Mansukh Brahman, who was at that time studying Russian in Kattakurgan. Mansukh gave him information about Ganga Ram. He also informed about the arrival in Samarkand on 18 September 1881 of Ghulam Rasul Lohani who left behind his two companions in Jammu and returned to Tashkent after ascertaining that Ibrahim Shah had really been sent to the Russian authorities by the Raja of Jaipur who was now dead and the state was being administered by the British whose tyranny resulted in widespread popular discontent. Ghulam Rasul Lohani had also contacted the Kukas and ascertained that Budh Singh and his followers were all waiting for their opportunity. According to the intelligence collected by the British agent Gulab Khan in Central Asia, which he communicated in his letter of 26 January 1882 through his Tadjik courier Mullah Ikram, the Russians wanted the Kashmir Maharaja to create trouble for the British when the fugitive Afghan Amir Abdur Rahman Khan returned to Kabul. But he also mentions the distrust of Russians by Abdur Rahman Khan who wanted the Russian escort of ten officers and 200 troopers not to accompany him beyond the Oxus.[55] Gulab Khan also informed the British about a letter of the Kuka Chief Budh Singh brought to Bukhara by Shambhu of Shikarpur and posted from there to General Abramov in Samarkand. According to the information obtained by Gulab Khan through Said Khan the letter carried the following message: "We are all ready and have also made preparations for war; we hope you will come quickly".[56]

Through his contact man Said Khan, Gulab Khan had undermined the prestige of the Kukas in the eyes of the Russian authorities and got one of their emissaries—Jas Ram Brahman—expelled from Samarkand. When the letter from the Kukas referred to above was received, the Russian started searching for Jas Ram. A special rider was sent to fetch him from Bukhara and General Abramov rewarded him with a *Khillat*. Jas Ram was despatched along with the Russian agent Ghulam Rasul Lohani to Jammu. Jas Ram also carried a letter from Mansukh Dogra. The reason for sending them to Jammu was to confirm the Kuka's claim of their enjoying the support of the Kashmir ruler.

Gulab Khan sent Mullah Ikram on their trail "in the hope that through him they might fall into government hands". He borrowed Rs. 150 at 6 per cent monthly interest from Ram Singh, a Shikarpuri moneylender, living at Kattakurgan to cover the expenses of Ikram's journey to India. Jas Ram was described by him as "a fat man of middle height, fair-complexioned with a grizzled beard, aged 45" and Ghulam Rasul as "an Afghan, very fair, of little above average height, with a black beard".

Gulab Khan's despatches and the statements of his courier Ghulam Mohiuddin also shed interesting light on the life and activities of Indian settlers in Central Asia in the early eighties of the nineteenth century. One can have an idea of the hostility of the Central Asian people against the Indian moneylenders from the incident of murder on 18 December 1881 of one Changu, a moneylender from Shikarpur, who lived for a long time at Kattakurgan and went to Kul Kurghan to realize a debt. The dead body of Changu lay for three days on the edge of the stream, wrote Gulab Khan. He also mentioned that the house of another Indian merchant, Abdulla Paracha of Rawalpindi district was broken into and tea and thread stolen. This merchant too was murdered in the same month of December 1881. Ghulam Mohiuddin in his statement, already cited, spoke about one Bakhsullah of Rampur then settled in Kattakurgan who fled from India during the 1857 revolt. Bakhsullah was a friend of Said Khan and came to Kattakurgan from Bukhara alongwith the latter. Later on Gulab Khan drove a wedge between the two friends. Gulab Khan's letter sent through Ghulam Mohiuddin also informed about one Maya Hindu who came to Balkh as a fugitive during the 1857 uprising. Gulab Khan also wrote about the Kattakurgan visit of Ram Chandra, the nephew of Nana Saheb, who came to Central Asia from St. Petersburg. But he mentioned him as "Ram Charan Tora, brother of Nana Rai". According to Gulab Khan's information the reply sent by the Russian Governor of Samarkand through Baba Karam Prakash, an Udasi Fakir, to the Maharaja of Kashmir in the early 1870s was to the effect that "Russians had no immediate intention of attacking Hindustan but that when they intended to come the Raja would be informed".[57] The letter of Gulab Khan sent through his agent Ghulam Mohiuddin referred to Jas Ram, a Brahmin of Patiala and Ilahi Bakhsh Mirasi as emissaries of the Kuka Chief Baba Budh Singh and his confidant Gurcharan Singh. Gulab Khan also informed the British that the Russian authorities at Samarkand were not "inclined to carry on any further correspondence with the Kukas".

The despatch of emissaries by the Kukas and Kashmir Durbar to Central Asia must have caused some anxiety to the British authorities in India. As Lord Clarendon had made it clear in his conversation with Prince Gortchakoff at Heidelberg in 1869 the British had no apprehensions of a Russian invasion of India and the "only apprehension we had was. . . that the nearer approach of the Russians and intrigues with native chiefs might keep the Indian mind in ferment and entail upon us much trouble and expense all of which would be avoided by a clear understanding with the Russian Government by which a neutral ground between the possessions of the two countries might be established".[58]

In the early seventies of the nineteenth century the British came to suspect Kashmir's contact with the Russian power in Central Asia. It was C.U. Aitchison, Secretary Foreign Department of Government of India, who drew attention to the rumours of Kashmir's correspondence with Russia which "point to the necessity of having a permanent Resident, the very best man we can get in Kashmir".[59] Aitchison wrote: "Imperial interests in that quarter are of such vast importance that we cannot go on longer in the dark as to what takes place beyond the Kashmir frontier."[60]

Lord Northbrook, the Viceroy and Governor-General of India, announced to the Maharaja of Kashmir his intention of establishing permanently a Resident at his Court in Srinagar. This step was taken in the wake of the Maharaja making known to the Government of India the overtures made to one Khalikdar, a Kashmiri at Yarkand, by a member of the Russian mission to open direct communication with the Maharaja. The British intelligence had reported the Kashmir ruler's increasing anxiety over the Russian advance in Central Asia leading to the appointment of a young Maulavi who pretended to know Russian lanuage to teach the young princes. The Maulavi proved to be an impostor and was dismissed when it was discovered that he was teaching a language of his own invention.[61] Mohammed Khan Effendi, a Circassian who had been in the military service of the Amir of Kashgar had told the Secretary to the Punjab Government that the Maharaja consulted him as to the best means of sending a letter and envoy to St. Petersburg explaining that he had received communications from General Kaufmann but he did not trust him and wished to deal directly with the Tsar.[62]

The Maharaja of Kashmir felt hurt by the British proposal to station a permanent Resident at Srinagar and protested against it to the Viceroy Lord Northbrook. A long correspondence on the subject followed between the two and ultimately Lord Northbrook agreed to the proposal made by the Maharaja that a British officer to Leh should remain there all the year round instead of only during the summer months as heretofore, and that an officer on special duty in Srinagar should stay there for eight months instead of six.[63]

British suspicions about the Kashmir Durbar's and Kukas' contacts with the Russians continued to linger on throughout the eighties of nineteenth century. Thus, the Punjab Special Branch in the confidential report of 14 July 1882 mentioned Sardar Ganda Singh in Jammu "who is said to have deputed two Kukas to Russian territory to enquire of Bishan Singh when the Russians would invade India and the *Khalsa Raj* be established". The District Superintendent of Police, Ludhiana, reported on 30 May 1885 that "Bishan Singh, the well-known Kuka Suba in Russian territory, visited Bhaini about two years ago". He was reported to have presented a *chogha* and portrait of the Emperor of Russia to Baba Budh Singh. On 4 December 1886, the District Superintendent of Police, Ferozepur, reported that a rumour was current in his district that Maharaja Dalip Singh was with the Russians and was accompanied by the Kuka Suba Bishan Singh. The Superintendent of Police, Jullunder reported that the Kukas became "very excited when talking of Dalip Singh, and performed the *Chandi-Ka-Path*". Suba Bishan Singh, the Kuka leader was believed to be staying in Central Asia along with his son-in-law Jaimal Singh and both were suspected to be in the Russian Secret Service. The eighty-year old Kuka emissary who was imprisoned on his return from his first Central Asian mission and freed in 1887 only was again reported to be planning to go to Tashkent in February 1889.

Sadhu Singh, who was reported to own land and houses at Kattakurgan and who resided there for twenty-one years was suspected by the British to have returned to Shikarpur with the aim of sending information to the Russians. In the records contained in the National Archives of India there is a reference to one "Paro, son of Hasa Nand, a friend of Gortchakoff and the late Kaufmann . . . now residing at his home Vada Vehra, Shirkarpur City". Paro was for about ten years at Tashkent where he "formed the acquaintance of Ram Chand Pradhan, a relative of famous Nana Rao, with whom he is still in correspondence".[64]

The Indian national movement felt the impact of the Russian conquest of Central Asia. F. Engels had written: ". . . When a first class European military power asserts itself in Turkistan, endeavours by a combination of force and cajolery to make Persia and Afghanistan into its vassals, and moves slowly but doggedly towards the Hindu Kush and the Sulayman range . . . there you have a very different state of affairs. British dominion ceases to be ineluctable fate, and a new perspective opens before the native population. What force has created force can also break as under . . ."[65]

On the eve of the Russian annexation of Central Asia many deserters from the British Indian Army had taken shelter in Bukhara and Kokand after the failure of the 1857 uprising. The Russian advance in Central Asia stirred the hopes of the Indian people to throw off the yoke of British colonial oppression. Of course, this hope was at first confined to a few rulers of princely states who had no popular aspirations and who merely sought to utilize the contradictions between the two colonial powers to their advantage.

Soviet historians N.A. Khalfin, G.L. Dmitriyev and P.N. Rasul'zade have written about the various missions sent by Indian princes to the Russian authorities in Turkistan to seek help against the British. Thus, Maharaja Ranbir Singh of Kashmir sent a mission of four persons soon after the Russian annexation of Tashkent. Two of the emissaries including the leader were murdered on the way and the letter from the Maharaja vanished with them. The two survivors, Abdur Rahman Khan and Sarfaraz Khan succeeded in reaching Tashkent in November 1865. They were received by General Chernyayev to whom they affirmed friendship of their ruler and inquired what might be expected of the Russians. The records of Central State Military History Archives of U.S.S.R. contain information about this mission.[66] The mission did not meet with any success. The Tsarist Government was not interested in promoting the cause of national liberation of India. It was interested in its colonial expansion only. For want of adequate material resources it did not at the moment feel inclined to involve itself in trouble with the mighty British Empire. In September 1866 another emissary from Kashmir who is mentioned in Russian records as Uromchan Davidas reached Alma Ata, the capital of Kazakh SSR. He was taken into Russian service and died in Taskhent a year later.[67]

In July 1867 another emissary from the Indian ruler of Indore came to Tashkent, who described himself as the son of the Chief Minister Gauhar Rahman of Indore State. He sought Russian help in the name of a number of princely states such as Hyderabad, Bikaner, Jodhpur and Jaipur.[68] The mission met a fate similar to the ones preceding it.

A second mission from Maharaja Ranbir Singh of Kashmir arrived in Tashkent in June 1870. It was headed by Baba Karam Prakash who conveyed the Maharaja's request for the establishment of political and trade relations. Karam Prakash told the Russians that the Maharaja of Kashmir had declined to go to Ambala where he was invited by Lord Mayo to join him in his meeting with the Afghan Amir Sher Ali.[69] The Russian colonial administration while treating these Indian missions with hospitality did not give them any official reply. It was keen to avoid running into difficulties with the British power in India.

In 1879 there arrived in Tashkent yet another mission from India, this time, a popular one. Gurcharan Singh, an old man in his seventies, brought a letter to the Russian Governor General from the head of the Namdhari (Kuka) Sikhs in Punjab. The letter was written by Ram Singh who had been arrested by the British in 1872 and kept in Rangoon jail. Ram Singh invited Russians to come to the Punjab to help its people in their fight against their British oppressors.[70]

General Kaufmann sent to St. Petersburg the letter brought by the Namdhari envoy. For the first time an official reply was given which, though courteous enough, was essentially evasive. As already noted above, British spy Gulab Khan informed the British of the visit of Gurcharan Singh who was arrested on his return to India and kept in prison for six years.

In April 1890, one Gulam Haidar Khan, who described himself as a relation of the former Nawab of Lucknow, came to Ashkhabad, capital of the Turkmen SSR. He claimed to have been sent by the King of Nepal. General Kuropatkin recommended to the Tsar that he be handed over an official letter when he went back. But the Foreign Ministry turned down this suggestion and he had to return without it.[71] The Central State Archives of Military History of U.S.S.R. also contain papers throwing light on the efforts of the Hunza ruler to establish close relations with the Russians in Central Asia. The Hunza emissaries were received by Vrevsky, the Governor General of Turkistan who conveyed his greetings to the ruler of this border state but refused to commit himself against the British. Russian Captain Grombchevsky was received with his Cossack escorts by the Hunza chieftain Safdar Ali in 1888. British Captain Younghusband met him in the Tagdumbash Pamir in October 1889. The second attempt by Grombchevksy in late 1889 to visit Hunza and Leh was foiled by the British who withheld permission to visit these places by a Russian officer. The British ultimately deposed Safdar Ali in 1891.

In the Moscow Archives of Foreign Policy of Russia is preserved an interesting despatch of 6 September 1903 from the Russian, Consul-General in Bombay, which speaks of the great discontent of the Indian people with the British rule and their deep sympathies for the Russian people. The Consul-General was receiving letters from educated young Indians who informed him that the whole of the Punjab has been waiting for the Russians to come. He wrote home about a widespread popular belief in India that Russia would come to liberate them from the British colonial rule.[72] An indication of the hopes pinned on Russian aid by Indian patriots is provided by Tilak's overtures to the Russian Consuls, Cherkin and Klemm in Bombay for sending Indian youths abroad for military training. Tilak also approached them for introductions to Russian firms in order to purchase machinery for the establishment of Indian factories.[73]

Just as missions from India went to Central Asia to seek Russian help, so did missions from Central Asia come to India to seek British help against the Russians. In the National Archives of India we find information concerning several such missions in the same period. In fact, the first mission from Central Asia arrived in India to seek British assistance against the Russians as early as 1854. Of course, much earlier towards the close of the eighteenth century and in the opening years of nineteenth century, a Central Asian, Gabidulla Amirov, had travelled across India from Bukhara to Calcutta and Dacca. Amirov travelled about 15,000 kilometres on foot in a journey extending over thirty years, which carried him to such Indian towns as Attock, Shikarpur, Sukkar, Hyderabad, Jaisalmer, Jodhpur, Jaipur, Delhi, Agra, Lucknow, Calcutta, Murshidabad, Dacca and to Ajmer, Ujjain, Aurangabad, Poona, Chittor, Bikaner, Nagore, Multan and Dera Gazi Khan, on his way back to Orenburg where he died in 1805.[74] Amirov's mission was however not of a political character.

But in August 1854 a Central Asian physician named Moolah Yar Mohamed arrived in Peshawar to "authenticate a Kokand envoy named Shahzada (Prince) Sooltan" who was despatched after the seizure of the fort of Ak Mesjid by the Russians advancing towards Central Asia. Yar Mohammed who reached Peshawar through

Badakhshan because of hostility between Kabul and Bukhara was identified by the peon of Major Edwardes, the Commissioner of Peshawar division – one Mahomed Ali who had been sent to Kokand by Col. Lawrence in 1849. The Khan of Kokand requested the Government of India to send European military instructors to train his forces. This request however did not find favour with either the Commissioner of Peshawar, Major Edwardes, or the Governor of the Punjab, John Lawrence, who considered the measure "impolitic and unwise" because of the "extreme" risk involved in it.[75] The Governor-General in Council nevertheless favoured sending of Muslim native officers possibly from the Western provinces provided they volunteered to go to Central Asia on their own responsibility.[76]

The Commissioner of Peshawar division, Major Edwardes was in two minds over the request of Kokand Khan for military instructors. He did not doubt "its sincerity or of the imminence of the danger with which the Kokand Kingdom is threatened". But he also desired that "the assistance be proportioned to the object and not calculated to involve us in military operations at a distance from our own territory."[77] Edwardes believed that the "English officers invited by the Khan would be perfectly safe" as the "feelings of the people towards us were more friendly than those of the Afghans before we spilt their blood and tried to denationalise their government". He wrote: "Had I not a wife to leave behind I should myself willingly go on such a duty; and think there was more of enterprise than of danger in it".[78] Finally the "forbidding shadow of the fate of Stoddart and Conolly in Bukhara and the fate of our army at Kabul" prevented him from agreeing to the proposition of leading half a dozen English Officers to a Kingdom in independent Tartary. He remained contented with "detailed intelligence from the envoy about the country from Kokand to Ak Mesjid and Peshawar". The Kokand envoy was interrogated at length by him at Peshawar about the state of roads, availability of fodder for the horses, water, etc.[79]

In his letter sent through the Kokand envoy in 1854 the Governor-General assured the Khan of Kokand that the "attacks with which the Powers are threatening Russia on every side will deter her for the present from entering on any projects of aggression elsewhere"[80] – he was referring to the Crimean War. He advised the Khan to strengthen his military preparedness and never to trust the promises of moderation held out by the Russians and commended the example of the resistance of the Circassian tribes against Russia's onslaught.

Another envoy from Kokand named Khoja Beg Ishak Ghazee reached India in 1864. The Kokand mission apprised the Viceroy, Sir John Lawrence of the difficulties of the Khan with the Amir of Bukhara and Russia. But the Viceroy regretted his inability to render any help on account of the "distance" and the "situation".[81] This was followed by yet one more mission from Kokand in 1865.[82] Its request for sending some experienced artillerymen was not met by the Virecroy.

The Amir of Bukhara too sent a mission to seek British aid in November 1866.[83] But like the previous missions from the Central Asian Khanates this mission also failed. A letter addressed from the ruler of Bukhara to the Queen of England was brought to Calcutta in January 1867 by an emissary, Khwaja Mahomed Parsa. It complained of the "Russian conduct and designs in Central Asia" and sought British help in expelling them (Russians)[64]. Parsa was the Chief Mufti of Bukhara. The Governor-General's reply was that "though willing to be on friendly terms the Government of India could not take cognizance of his alleged grievances against the Russians".[85]

The eldest son of the Amir of Bukhara who stirred up a revolt against his father after his signing up a treaty with the Russians, came to Peshawar in 1880 through Kashgar and Kabul. Prince Abdul Malik Tora arrived in Peshawar on 2 March 1880 accompanied by his two sons, eighteen wives and maidservants.[86] He was sanctioned a monthly allowance of Rs 1,175 by the Foreign Secretary. The Kokand Prince Syud Abdul Karim who had been staying at Peshawar since August 1878 received a daily allowance of Rs 40, which led to a demand by the Bukharan prince to increase his allowance. But this request of his was not conceded by the Government of India which advised the Peshawar Commissioner to reduce the allowance of the other Central Asia prince. Tora's application for a loan of Rs. 9,000 was also refused.[87] He was not allowed to accept the throne of Darwaz, a principality north of Badakhshan where the people invited him to become their ruler in 1882. His request for permission to visit Bukhara following his father's death in 1885 was also not granted by Sir Aitchison, the Lt. Governor of Punjab and Lord Dufferin, the Viceroy in February 1886.[88] The British feared a Russian thrust to the south as a reaction to any northward move by the Bukhara prince living in exile.

Likewise the British wrote to the Afghan Amir Abdul Rahman Khan in January 1882 cautioning against "disadvantage and risk" of interference in the affairs of a distant state like Khiva "under the present circumstances". The ruler and the people of Khiva had sent a letter dated 1 July 1881 to the British authorities through their agents Mirza Karawal Begi and Hakim Chibra Akassi offering to rise against the Russians when the British troops reached Herat[89].

The Central Asian missions and the Indian missions though had certain similarities in their objectives and nature, cannot be given equal importance. Whereas the Indian missions were backed by a popular upsurge against the British the same was not true regarding the Central Asian missions which were singularly of feudal origin. Even the Indian missions despatched by feudal princes were more broadbased in character and enjoyed a wider measure of popular support than their Central Asian counterparts. A popular mission like that of Gurcharan Singh from India never came from Central Asia. There was a vast difference in the extent and size of the national liberation movement in India and Central Asia. A major national uprising in Central Asia against Tsarist Russia did not take place until 1916, whereas India had uprisings against British colonial rule as far back as 1857.

The British continued to use every possible opportunity to collect intelligence from Central Asia. The miscellaneous news-letters and diaries received by Col. J.W. Ridgeway during his work as Her Majesty's Commissioner for the Delimitation of the Afghan Frontier in 1885-86 were sent to H.M. Durand, Secretary, Foreign

Department. These contained intelligence about Ashkhabad, Merv and even distant Tashkent and Bukhara collected by native agents like Munshi Alla Baksh, Mohammed Aslam Khan, and Sardar Sher Ahmad Khan.[90] Ridgeway's papers gave information about the state of roads in Tashkent and the break-up of guns—mounted and lying on the ground—at Bukhara.

The tradition of collecting detailed intelligence about Russian Central Asia was continued by British authorities in India even after the establishment of the Soviet power. The General Staff of India compiled this intelligence for official use in secret publication called *Military Report of Russian Turkistan*. The first edition of this classified document came out in 1905 followed by second and third editions in 1911 and 1914 respectively. Subsequently updated editions appeared in 1921 and 1931. These editions are preserved in the Library of the National Archives of India. This publication contains detailed information about the Russian army, garrison towns and fortresses and seaports, communications, roads, railways, waterways, telegraphs, etc. The 1914 edition of *Military Report on Russian Turkistan* includes the following significant remark about the Russian rule in Central Asia: "The Asiatic dislike for the European seems less marked, however, in Russian Turkistan than elsewhere in Asia. . . It is improbable that the natives as a whole, will ever rise against Russians".[91]

The rise of Soviet power in Central Asia following the victorious October Socialist Revolution led to intensified British efforts directed at sabotage and military intervention from India against the new revolutionary regime. The Government of India launched a big anti-Bolshevik propaganda and raised the bogey of military threat to the empire from the side of the Soviet power. The British launched their offensive against the Soviet power in Central Asia in the summer of 1918. It was a two-pronged drive with the Kashgar mission led by Lt. Col. Bailey organizing disruption in Tashkent from inside Turkistan and Major-General W. Malleson sending military and financial assistance to the Ashkhabad counter revolutionary government from Mashad. British writings on the subject have characterized stories about Bailey's activities in Central Asia in inspiring, organizing and coordinating opposition to the Soviet regime as 'a legend'[92] not fully supported by documentary evidence.

Facts, however, present an entirely different picture. The memoirs of the members of the Kashgar Mission, Bailey's own Report and the despatches of General Malleson preserved in the National Archives of India contain weighty and incontrovertible evidence indicting the British actions in Central Asia.

Let us first take the Report of the Kashgar Mission.[93] The mission consisted of Lt. Col. Bailey, Major Etherton and Captain Blacke₁ who were accompanied by Prince Abdur Rahim Beg of Kokand (whose family had taken refuge in India when the Russians annexed the Khanate) and some Indian non-commissioned Officers of the Guides. Leaving Kashgar towards the end of July 1918 it left behind Major Etherton at Kashgar as he was to replace Sir George Macartney as the Consul General there. We also learn from the Report that due to the leakage of the identity of Prince Beg "it was thought advisable to leave him behind in Kashgar lest the Russians should think that we contemplated making trouble for them in Kokhand".[94] The mission took as interpreter, Khan Sahib Iftekhar Ahmed the head clerk of the Kashgar Consulate General. Blacker returned to India in September 1918 leaving only Bailey and Iftekhar Ahmed in Tashkent.

Bailey writes in the Report: "Soon after my arrival I got into touch with what I judged to be the Chiefs of several anti-Bolshevik organizations".[95] He mentions in particular the anti-Bolshevik organization headed by General Kondratovitch, which also counted on the support of Argash. Bailey admits that he had planned to go to Farghana with General Kondratovitch to meet the Basmachi Chief Argash. He also writes that he believed that the British force in Trans-Caspia would advance "in which case it would be both more useful and safer. . .to remain in Tashkent until they arrived".[96] He had also "hoped to send news out that would be useful".

Etherton, who was also connected with the mission of Bailey to Tashkent, links it to the object of probing the Muslim autonomy movement in Central Asia. The British were then toying with the idea of creating a Muslim federation consisting of Afghanistan, autonomous Turkistan and the Caucasus.[97]

Captian Blacker's reminiscences also throw light on the real character of Bailey's mission to Tashkent. According to him there was no use collecting information which could not be transmitted soon enough to be useful. The mission, according to his version, was facing difficulties in sending message to Kashgar from where it was to reach Simla through Gilgit. "Some thirty to forty messengers, he complains, "had taken our money and slipped our messages into their great jackboots without tangible results"[98] The *Report on the Kashgar Mission 1918-20* mentions that the mission had brought a number of carrier pigeons "merely served to nourish the numerous hawks on the road."[99]

General Malleson had a sinister plan to execute from Mashad. The end of the war in November 1918 had taken away the alibi of preventing Central Asian cotton and Austro-Hungarian war prisoners from being used against the Allied cause. He now came out with his plan for the repatriation of the German and Austro-Hungarian prisoners of war held by the Bolsheviks in Central Asia as the first step towards arranging a referendum on the future form of government there. He confided this plan in an interview with Dorer, a member of the Ashkhabad counter-revolutionary government. Malleson was working on the presumption that the war prisoners formed the "chief asset" of the Bolsheviks and the movement would collapse if these could be got away".[100] The Government of India's concern for economy and its cautious approach against getting too deeply involved in the affairs of a distant land came in the way of a policy of liberal financial and military aid to the anti-Bolshevik Ashkhabad Government.

Contrary to false claims by General Malleson in his articles published from 1922 to 1933[101] that the British Mission even tried to save the twenty-six Commissars of Baku and the assertion made by C.H. Ellis[102] that the Bolshevik Commissars were executed by Russian SRs without the knowledge or consent of the British Mission to Trans-Caspia, the documents preserved in the National Archives of India prove beyond any doubt that the report about the Commissars' arrest was received by General Malleson from Col. Batino on 17 September 1918 itself and that they were arrested by the British themselves. The Chief of the General Staff at Simla wanted Malleson to take over the Bolshevik prisoners and hold them as hostages. But the latter informed him that "the men mentioned are already executed" and that if it was really so important to hold hostages he could "get others from the Ashkhabad Government" though "all of real importance have been shot." Not only this, Malleson cynically expressed his satisfaction over the execution of the twenty-six Baku Commissars. In his telegram dated 23 September 1918 he wrote: "I can express no opinion as to the question of justice, but apart from this the alleged execution is politically advantageous as it means Ashkhabad Government have burnt their boats as regards Bolsheviks. The political fence-sitters at Ashkhabad would have regarded Shaumian, Petrov and company as counters wherewith to save their own skins so long as the latter had remained alive".[103]

After the liberation of Central Asia by the Great October Socialist Revolution in 1917 this region became a centre of attraction for many Indian freedom fighters who made Tashkent a nucleus of their revolutionary activities. While the work of Indian revolutionaries in London, Paris, Berlin, Stockholm, New York, San Francisco and California in the West and Tokyo in the East is fairly well known, not much is known about their activities nearer home in Soviet Asia in the period immediately following the October Revolution.

During the First World War many nationalist revolutionaries left India to seek the assistance of foreign powers arrayed against Britain. As Tsarist Russia was an ally of Britain, there was no question of their approaching her for help. In 1915 the Indian Revolutionary Committee in Berlin included Raja Mahendra Pratap and Barkatullah in the Hentig mission sent to Afghanistan by the Imperial Germany to win over the Amir as an ally against Britain. In Kabul, Raja Mahendra Pratap established the "Provisional Government of India" with himself as the President, Barkatullah as the Prime Minister, and Obeidullah Sindhi as the Home Minister. Despite his German adviser Hentig's advice, the Raja proceeded to seek aid from Tsarist Russia as well. He was somewhat hopeful because of old Anglo-Russian antagonism in this region, though he was soon to get disillusioned. The Tsarist Russian authorities at Tashkent did not respond to his "Gold Plate Letter" to the Tsar and the two envoys he sent to Tashkent the second time were arrested and handed over to the British in Iran who executed them.

But if Tsarist Russia had snubbed all efforts of Indian revolutionaries to forge a link with it, the Soviet power readily welcomed those who wished to work for the liberation of India. It openly espoused the cause of all oppressed peoples of the East. The Montagu-Chelmsford Report on Indian Constitutional Reforms (1918) frankly admitted that the Revolution in Russia "has given impetus to Indian political aspirations". There were several thousand Indian settlers in the various cities of Central Asia, who provided a good base for anti-British activities from a region in close proximity to India. Moreover, escape to this region through uninhabited mountain passes was relatively safer than escape to Europe by sea. Hence, a steady stream of Indian patriots began to flow into Soviet Asia in the wake of the October Socialist Revolution.

Beginning with 1918 up to 1920 several groups of Indians reached Central Asia to seek Soviet help for the liberation of India. In February 1918 Mahendra Pratap arrived in Tashkent on the invitation of the Turkistan Soviet authorities and proceeded to Petrograd where he was received by high Government leaders. From Petrograd Mahendra Pratap went to Berlin. Following him several representatives of the "Provisional Government of India" in Kabul came to the Soviet Union. Besides the Central Asian cities of Tashkent and Bukhara, they also lived and worked in Moscow and Kazan and were particularly helpful to the young Soviet diplomacy in establishing contacts with Afghanistan.

Barkatullah came to Moscow through Tashkent in March 1919 after Amanullah had become the Amir of Afghanistan. He was entrusted by the new Amir the task of establishing permanent diplomatic relations with the Soviet Russia. On 7 May 1919 he was received by Lenin. On hearing of the war between Britain and Afghanistan he decided to return to Afghanistan from Moscow. According to Soviet historian M.A. Persits, Mahendra Pratap was back in Moscow in July 1919 accompained by Abdur Rab and Prativadi Acharya. Barkatullah met him there. Soon after Mahendra Pratap's arrival a delegation led by him and consisting of Barkatullah, Abdur Rab, Prativadi Achayra, Dalip Singh Gill and Ibrahim, a peasant from the Punjab, was received by Lenin. Mahendra Pratap in his negotiations with the Soviet Foreign Commisariat demanded recognition by the Soviet Government of his "Provisional Government of India" established at Kabul as the only centre of revolutionary forces of India. He also suggested a plan for Soviet-Afghan military expedition to liberate India.

A special mission of the "Provisional Government of India" at Kabul consisting of Mohammad Ali and Shafiq Ahmad arrived in Tashkent on 31 March 1920. They were later joined by Ibrahim and Abdul Majid. These people with Barkatullah as their leader formed the 'Provisional Government' group. This group stressed the expulsion of the British from India by a foreign military expedition, though it also talked of organizing a national army; Barkatullah conducted propaganda work in favour of the Soviet power among the Turkish war prisoners and the Muslim population in the Volga region and Central Asia and wrote a number of pamphlets depicting Bolshevism as a friend of Islam and bringing out the similarity between their social ideals and principles. The thinking of Barkatullah's group evolved towards the left and socialist ideas and several of its members actively worked for the Soviet of International Propaganda established in December 1919 in Tashkent by the Turkistan Commission of the Central Executive Committee. The tasks of this organization was to unite the various revolutionary organizaitons working on the territory of Soviet Turkistan with those working in the adjacent countries. The Indian section of the 'Sovinterprop' (Soviet of International Propaganda) sent some Indians to Baku and Iran to work among soldiers of the British Indian Army and to the Pamirs for work among the frontier tribes. It also brought out a number of pamphlets and brochures. One issue of its weekly called *Zamindar* appeared from Tashkent.

A new and bigger group of organized Indian nationalist revolutionaries arrived in Tashkent from Kabul on 2 July 1920. It was led by Abdur Rab and had a strength of twenty-eight. They had already organized themselves in Kabul as the Indian Revolutionary Association. The Association had sent from Kabul a message of greetings to Lenin to which he sent an inspiring reply. A public reception was arranged in their honour in Tashkent, which was attended by such high Soviet dignitaries as V.V. Kuibyshev and M.V. Frunze. Among the members of the Indian Revolutionary Association there were ten to twelve British army deserters. The two Nasir Khan brothers, leaders of the independent Baluch tribes who had risen against the British in 1917-18, were also among those who came to Tashkent along with Abdur Rab. Prativadi Acharya also accompanied the group. Seven members of the Indian Revolutionary Association were among the fourteen Indian delegates who participated in the Baku Congress of the Peoples of the East held in September 1920. The members of Association thought in terms of liberation of India by Soviet Russia with the support of independent tribal frontiermen. There were in Soviet Tashkent about 100 Indian fighters against British Imperialism. The number rose to nearly 200 by December 1920. The Turkbureau of the Comintern informed the Central Executive Committee about the arrival of groups of Indian Khilafat emigrants. In Bukhara too a number of Indian emigrants including about twenty Bengalis arrived in late 1920 and early 1921.

M.N. Roy and Abani Mukherjee reached Tashkent on October 1, 1920. The news of the arrival of a large number of Khilafat emigrants brought them to Central Asia. They saw in it an opportunity for forming the nucleus of a liberation army which was to be organized in Afghanistan from out of the tribal frontiermen of India who nurtured strong anti-British feelings. Roy came to Tashkent after having formed in Moscow itself, All-India Provisional Central Revolutionary Committee consisting of the Indian participants of the Second Congress of the Comintern. While paying lip service to the Leninist line of forging a united front of anti-imperialist forces as adopted at the Second Congress, Roy did not abandon his negative position in relation to co-operation with not only national bourgeoisie but also national revolutionary organizations. His Revolutionary Committee soon came into clash with the Indian Revolutionary Association headed by Abdur Rab and Acharya. In early December, Abdur Rab who had been opted as a member of the Revolutionary Committee was expelled from the organization. The differences between Roy and Abdur Rab became so acute that the Turkbureau of the Central Committee and the Executive Bureau of the Communist Party of Turkistan in a joint meeting on 31 December 1920 asked them to go to Moscow for solving them.

During his brief stay in Tashkent, Roy came face to face with the practical difficulties of organizing the Communist movement in the East. He had not been thus far cognizant of these problems and considered the task of establishment of the hegemony of the proletariat over the national struggle for liberation from the British rule as a realistic one. But his failure to make a good number of Khilafat emigrants agree to receive political and ideological training in Tashkent taught him a lesson. Even the attraction of receiving military training did not win him many adherents. The Military School at Tashkent was joined by only twenty-five Indian emigrants by the end of 1920 and the maximum number rose to thirty-nine in March 1921 after which it began to decline. In May 1921 the School was wounded up and its Indian trainees were sent to Moscow to study at the Communist University of the Toilers of the East. Later some of them were arrested by the British on their arrival in India and tried in Peshawar Conspiracy Case and were sentenced to various terms of imprisonment. The plan to organize an Indian Liberation Army at Tashkent suffered a setback also on account of refusal of the Afghan Government to give permission to cross its territory on way to India. Even otherwise the plan of accomplishing a socio-political revolution in India mainly by an outside military expedition was highly impractical. It smacked of petty-bourgeoisie revolutionism.

During the Soviet period the Central Asian people who were earlier mere pawns on the chessboard of imperialist rivalry between Tsarist Russia and Britain came into their own. Their segregation from the neighbouring countries had become a thing of the past and they were successfully developing, as free and equal Republics of the U.S.S.R., and have closer friendly relations with them. The attainment of independence by India in 1947 also paved the way for a new phase of relations with the people of Central Asia.

REFERENCES

1. See R.C. Majumdar, *British Paramountcy and Indian Renaissance*, Vol. 1, 1963, pp. 1039-1044; Bisheshwar Prasad, *The Foundations of India's Foreign Policy*, Vol. 1, 1955, p. 263; also K.K. Datta's foreword to V. Terway's book, *East India Company and Russia* (1800-1857). New Delhi, 1977.

2. William Moorcroft and George Trebeck, *Travels in the Himalyan Provinces of Hindustan and the Punjab, in Ladakh and Kashmir in Peshawar, Kabul, Kunduz and Bokhara*, Vol. 2, pp. 471-73 also p. 454.

3. *Ibid.*, p. 466.

4. *Foreign Department, General B. Progs.*, Jan. 1872, Nos. 329/331; *Capt. P.D. Henderson's Translation of Travels in Central Asia by Meer Izzut-oolah in the years 1812-13*, p. 55.

5. *Ibid.*, p. 60.

6. *Ibid.*, p. 61.

7. *Ibid.*, p. 64.

8. *Ibid.*, pp. 69-70.

9. *AVPR, F. Spb. Glav Arkhiv, II-26, 1811, D-4, L. 11-12.*

10. *Ibid.*

11. *AVPR, F. Spb. Glav Arkhiv, II-3, 1811, D-5, L-12.*

12. Moorcroft to C.T. Metcalfe, 6 May 1821, Moorcroft, *Travels*, Vol. 1, p. 283.

13. V. Bartold, *Istoriya Izucheniya Vostoka: v Evrope i v Rossii*, Moscow 1928, p. 228.

14. *Foreign Department Secret,* 25 November 1831, No. 3.
15. *Ibid.*
16. *Ibid.*
17. *Ibid.*
18. A. Burnes, *Travels into Bukhara: Being the Account of a Journey from India to Cabool, Tartary and Persia,* Vol. 1, London, 1834, p. 347.
19. *Ibid.,* p. 299.
20. *Ibid.,* p. 277.
21. *Ibid.,* p. 258.
22. *Ibid.*
23. *Ibid.,* p. 298.
24. *Ibid.,* p. 273.
25. Mohan Lal, *Travel in the Punjab, Afghanistan and Turkestan to Balkh, Bokhara and Herat and a Visit to Great Britain and Germany,* London, 1846, pp. 150-51.
26. *Ibid.,* pp. 138-39, 162.
27. H. Rawlinson, *England and Russia in the East,* London, 1875, pp. 153-54.
28. A. Vambery, *History of Bokhara,* London, 1873, pp. 384-88.
29. H. Rawlinson, *op. cit.,* p. 152.
30. *Ibid.,* pp. 182-83.
31. See N.A. Khalfin, *Politika Rossii v Srednei Azii,* Moscow, 1960, p. 47.
32. *Ibid.*
33. Indra Singh Rawat, *Indian Explorers of the 19th Century,* Publications Division: Ministry of Information and Broadcasting, New Delhi, 1973, p. xv.
34. *Travels in Central Asia,* Punjab State Archives, Patiala, M/357/4346/ p. 23.
35. *Ibid.,* p. 24.
36. *Ibid.,* pp. 36-37.
37. *Foreign Department, Pol. B Progs. November 1871.* No. 31.
38. *Ibid.,* p. 1.
39. *Ibid.,* p. 7.

40. *Ibid.*, p. 29.
41. *Ibid.*, p. 30.
42. *Ibid.*, pp. 17-20.
43. *Ibid.*, p. 19.
44. *Foreign Department Pol. A., June 1866*, Nos. 171/173.
45. *Ibid.*
46. *Foreign Department Pol. A., K.W., Proceedings, November 1868, Nos. 1-4.* "Trade with Central Asia, Proposed Negotiations with Russia."
47. *Ibid.*
48. *Foreign Department, Secret, August 1876, Nos. 56-57, News-Letter from F.B.*
49. *Ibid.*
50. *Foreign Department, Pol. A, Proceedings January 1868, No. 89.*
51. *Ibid.*
52. *Foreign Department, Secret, August 1882, No. 351.*
53. *Foreign Department, Secret, August 1882, Nos. 349-359.*
54. *Ibid.*, No. 356.
55. *Ibid.*
56. *Ibid.*
57. *Ibid.*
58. *Foreign Department, Secret, Home Branch 1869, 94/96.*
59. *Foreign Department, Secret, Home Branch, 1869, 94/96 K.W. Sec., March 1875, Nos. 19-29.*
60. *Ibid.*
61. *Correspondence between Kashmir and Trans-Frontier States other than Kabul, Foreign Department, Secret, 1879, Nos. 829/30A.*
62. *Ibid*
63. *Foreign Department, Secret, March 1875, Nos. 19-29. Central Asian Affairs and Appointment of a Permanent Resident in Cashmere.*
64. *Extracts from Thugee and Dacoity Department, Special Branch, Abstracts of Intelligence, Vol. 2 (Calcutta, 4th March 1889), No. 10, Political Movements, Sects, Leaders & Co.*
65. K. Marx and F. Engels, *Sochineniya* T. XVI, Ch. II, p. 34.
66. *Ts. GVIA SSSR, F. 483, D. 95.*

67. *Ts. GVIA SSR, VUA, F. 483.*

68. *Ts. GAUz. SSSR, F. 7 5, op 35, D. 2.*

69. *Ts. GAUz., SSR, F. KTGG, op. 34, D-25, L. 20-22.*

70. *Ts. GAUz SSR, F. KTGG, op. 34, F. 462, L. 89.*

71. *Ts. GVIA SSSR*, F. 400, op. 261/911, D. 51.

72. *AVPR, F. Sredne-Aziatskii Stol, 1903*, No. 922, L. 106-109.

73. *Source Material for a History of the Freedom Movement in India*, II, pp.215-16; also A.V. Raikov, "Anglo-Indiiskaya Armiya natsional' no-osvoboditelniya dvizheniye v Indii v 1905-1907 godakh", *Problemy Vostokovedeniya*, No. 2, Moscow, 1959, p. 129.

74. *Proceedings of the Russian Geographical Society*, Book X, St. Petersburg, 1855, pp. 354-373.

75. *Foreign Department, Secret A., November 1854, Nos., 1-22*, p. 107.

76. *Ibid.*, p. 177.

77. *Ibid.*, pp. 35-37.

78. *Ibid.*

79. *Ibid.*, p. 209.

80. *Ibid.*, p. 119.

81. *Foreign Department, Pol. A, Dec. 1864, Nos. 238-240.*

82. *Foreign Department, Pol. A. Feb. 1865, Nos. 151/154.*

83. *Foreign Department, Pol. Progs., 869, No. 65.*

84. *Foreign Department, Pol., Despatch to Secretary of State, 24 January 867*, No. 19.

85. *Ibid.*

86. *Foreign Department, Secret, June 1880, Nos. 139-144*, No. 143.

87. *Foreign Department, Frontier A., Dec. 1887, Nos. 1-10.*

88. *Foreign Department, Secret-F., February 1886*, Nos. 60-70.

89. *Foreign Department, Secret, February 1882*, Nos. 24-32.

90. *Foreign Department, Secret-F., May 1886*, Nos. 39-97.

91. *Military Report on Russian Turkistan*, General Staff India, 1914, pp. 27-28. (Third Edition).

92. See "The Revolt in Transcaspia 1918-1919", By a Correspondent, *Central Asian Review*, 1954, Vol. VII, No. 2, pp. 117-130.

93. *Report of the Kashgar Mission 1918-1920. Foreign and Political Deptt., Secret-External Proceedings, August 1920*, Nos. 253-256.

94. *Ibid.*, p. 1.

95. *Ibid.*, p. 3.

96. *Ibid.*, p. 24.

97. See P.T. Etherton, *In the Heart of Asia*, London, 1925, p. VII.

98. L.V.S. Blacker, *On Secret Patrol in High Asia,* London, 1922, p. 32.

99. *Report on the Kashgar Mission, 1918-20*, p. 1.

100. *Telegram P. No. 15733, dated 21st November 1918 from the Viceroy to the Secretary of State, London.*

101. See W. Malleson, 'The British Military Mission to Turkestan 1918-1920" in *Journal of the Central Asia Society,* Vol. IX, 1922; also his article 'The Twenty-six Commissars' in *Fortnightly Review,* March, 1933.

102. C.H. Ellis, *The Trans-Caspian Episode,* London, 1963.

103. *Foreign and Political Department, External, Part B, Secret Proceedings, November 1922, Nos. 33-94*, p. 2.

7

An Essay on the Ethnography of a Group of Indic Language Speaking Pariah (in the Hissar Valley)*

I.M. Oranskii

The author met seven groups of pariah in the Central Asian part of the Hissar valley and the upper reaches of Surkhan Darya extending from the suburbs of Dushanbe in the north-east to the region of Sary-Asiya-Denau in south-west in Uzbekistan SSR.

A major section of the Pariah is concentrated within the limits of present-day region of Hissar (including the former Shahrinausi) of Tajikstan. Moving towards south-west the number of pariah gradually keeps on decreasing and outside Sary-Asiya-Denau only isolated families live. Pariah live in small groups (usually from 3-4 up to 15-20 families) all related to each other either by ties of marriage or kinship. They are spread all over the area and can hardly be distinguished from the surrounding Uzbek or Tajik population. In the above-mentioned territory there is no sector with a compact population of the pariah. In the Uzbek part of the Tadjik Villages pariah families live together, as a rule, in isolated quarters. This is evident in village Afgono, near the settlement Langari Bolo (Village

---

* I.M. Oranskii, "K etnografii indoyazichnoi, gruppy parya [Gissarskaya dolina]" in D.A. Oldderogge (chief editor), *Strany i Narody Vostoka Indiya - Strana i Narod*, Kniga II, Moskva, 1972, pp. 219-233.

Soviet Khanaka of the Hissar region) and others. According to author's calculation and information collected from informants there are between 200 and 250 households of the pariah and so the number of the group would be around 1000. Presently, majority of the members of this group along with the local population generally work in cotton-producing kolkhozes. The pariah are not distinguished from the surrounding population in terms of dress, food, types of housing, life-style, religious beliefs (they follow the Sunni faith of the Muslims), etc. Their children study in Uzbek and Tadjik schools.

The pariah are generally bilingual (native Indo-Aryan dialect and the Tajik language in any of its regional variation). In the family, in the household and among the circle of relatives, the language of intercourse is their native dialect. Despite their small numbers and their being bilingual and the Tajik and Uzbek surroundings, the use of native dialect in the family by this group of pariah is very common. Having lived for some time with different families of this group, I can affirm that even the smallest child who had just started speaking, would talk exclusively in the native language and would only later on start learning Uzbek or Tajik or both as the case might be. Even in mixed families where the father is a pariah and the mother a Tajik, the child first learns to speak his native dialect, thanks to strong ties with the relatives of the father. The author met families where the Tajik women (in one case an Uzbek woman) after marriage to a member of this pariah group, soon learnt to speak this dialect.

Outside the family and the circle of close relatives, the language in everyday use is Tajik, a language which is spoken by all the members of the group including the women. Many men (especially living in regions and Kolkhozes where the Uzbek population is dominant) also speak the Uzbek language. Young men who are students more or less freely speak Russian.

There is no script of the language and the pariah's memory of his past does not go beyond one or two generations beyond the oldest living member. According to their view the basic activity of this group was agriculture (*kistukor*), especially the cultivation of tobacco *temokukori*) and horticulture. Among grains, they sowed wheat (*gandúm*), rice (*šalí*) and in melonfields and gardens they planted onions (*piyóz*) and brinjal (*bengá*). They did keep cattle but cattle-rearing was not the chief branch of their economic activity. The pariah never practised crafts and did not participate in manufacturing activities.

The pariah came to Central Asia from Afghanistan. Nothing definite can be said about the timing of their arrival. It seems that different sections or even different families of this group did not arrive here simultaneously. In respect of some families, it can be said that the grandfathers of the oldest of middle-aged members of present families had lived in Central Asia; others probably came later. Sometimes families changed their places of residence moving from one place in Central Asia to another or even from one place to another in Afghanistan.

The pariah consider Lagman[1] (Lagmon) as their place of origin. It is situated between Kabul and Jalalabad.[2] According to old members, many families of their relations stay in Lagman, especially in the section called Kalu.[3] Some also live in the region of Kabul, Hanabad, Talikana. In these places lived other sections of this group as well.

Old representatives, especially of middle generation know from hearsay about other towns and places in Afghanistan (Jalalabad, Khanabad, Balkh, Mazar-i-sharif, Andhkhui, Gulbahar, Bulyagaii)[4] where members of this group are to be found. They know of rivers Kabul, Ghorband, Khazhdanahar[5], Gilmend[6] and about Afghans (Pashtun), tribals Ghilzai (haljai), safi, durrani (durranái).

Their memories of India appear to be still more far-fetched and confused. They remember the names of Multan, Peshawar and remember (not all) that their forefathers were connected with India and their native tongue is also connected with India.

The most important fact that emerges is that the pariah strongly held the belief that their ancestors were disciples of Sheikh Shamsi Tabrizi (Hazrati Shams)[7] — a name whose legends and miracles are associated with India. My informants told me that his grave is situated in India. The representatives of the members of this group and other migrants from Afghanistan, especially the members of Kabul group (sheh-momadi)[8] also associate themselves with Shams Tabrizi. Eighty-year old Bozor-boi, migrant from Rustak (north Afghanistan) observed that members of his group sometimes named themselves after their pri-Tabrizi.[9] The legend is widely prevalent that the sun came down from the sky so as to roast his meat at the request of Shams Tabrizi. In Tajik text of the legend written and preserved in one of the villages of group Kabol (Sheh-momadi)[10], the group of pariah is twice described as Hindustani (hindustoniyo). There can be no doubt that the text is a variant of the legend about Sheikh Shams Tabrizi whose activities are detailed in literature about Multan.[11]

Another story was also heard — which is not so legendary about a pir who lived on the outskirts of Regar, probably in the living memory of the present generation, to whom the pariah presented gifts.[12] The story is told that as a child he asked his father to take him to *buzkasi*, but his father did not accede to his request. He then saddled a horse and galloped after his father.

As has been already stated, the believing pariah profess Sunnite Islam. The city of Mazar-i-Shariff in north Afghanistan where the tomb of their holyman (*avliya*) exists is well-known to them. In the past this was a place of pilgrimage to them.[13] The tomb is called Mazor-i-Sakhi *i.e.* "generous benefactor and curative tomb". The old among the pariah hold that the worship of the tomb enables one to escape from different diseases. The land around the tomb is also supposed to hold curative properties. The pilgrims bring home the earth from the place for their near and dear ones. Mazar-i-Shariff is often mentioned in their folk-lores.[14]

Fairy tales, folk-lores and anecdotes in the dialect of the pariah basically have subjects, well-known to the repertoire of fairy tales of other people in Central Asia.[15] It is as yet not possible to draw any significant information from them about the past of the pariah. It should be noted that in these tales there are references to India (Hindustan) and Hindus (Hindu) which reflect the memories of the customs of Hindus and Hindu-Muslim relations.[16] Stories on subjects such as "King Sultan"[13, Text No. 1] and "King Sanavara and his unfaithful wife Gul"[13, Text No. III and XV] are well known in the writings of Persian as well as in Urdu and in other Indian languages. The kernel of the subject matter and the characters of the tale "Patykhan and Karamai" [13, Text No. XVIII] is well known in the corresponding Afghan fairy tale translated into Russian as "Fateh Khan Baretsai".[17] This fairy-tale is interesting because of the introduction of 'Beits' in a fixed singing style sung by the story-teller not in the dialect of the pariah but in the Afghan language Pashto. The preservation of these 'Beits' points to the fact that the basic text has been borrowed from the Afghan language Pashto and rendered into pariah dialect and so the 'Beits' in the original Pashto have been allowed to exist.[18] In the other tales published in the above-mentioned collection of folk-lores (No. II, V, XIII), it has not been possible to discover any close variation of the subject matter.

Folk-lores in songs do not exist in the pariah dialect. As has been shown the 'Beits' interpolated in the fairy-tales of pariah dialects are to be sung in Pashto. The lyrical gazals and song (*git*) are sung in Pashto. But the representatives of this group of pariah do not know Pashto. The meaning of the 'Beits' and 'songs' which have been memorised are known to the performers only in outlines. The lyrical gazals and songs are sung with the accompaniment of a double-stringed instrument *[dum(b)ra,* in Tajik *dumbri]*. This melody is not to be found among the local population.[19]

The pariah group consists of a number of branches (*qom, urur*) of which in course of researches the following were found: Kalu (kalu, kalo), Jitan (Jitan, jitiyan), Juni (juni), Magar (magara), bisiyan (bisyan, bisyon), musalli (musli, musalli). The branch shuya (suya) was also mentioned. After 1930s, not a single family of Shuya remained in Central Asia. The core of this group consists of the first four branches mentioned above which is jointly mentioned as "Shahi-khel" (šahi-khel),: *mo cor bob* šahi-khel-kalu, juni, jitan, magara— "We are shahi-khel consisting of four branches : Kalu, juni, jitan, magara."[20] The section kalu was the largest among these branches, living in the Hissar valley. Families belonging to the branches of juni, jitan and magara are rarely met.

The branch bisiyan somewhat stands by itself and is usually found with the group kabol (sheh-momadi)[21]. Bisiyan think that their forefathers came to Central Asia from Lagman and Talikan (Tolakon). Members of the kalu branch noted that bisiyan do not speak 'pure' pariah language. In fact, both the representative of bisiyan with whom I worked gave the firm impression that they did not have mastery over this dialect. It is, however, not clear whether this is the result of gradual loss of dialect by the bisiyan branch of pariah or the result of the fact that this is not their mother tongue and they learnt it from other branches.

The author met one of the two persons belonging to the other pariah group *musalli* residing in the village Khanaka in the Hissar region.[22] However, both appeared to be of mixed breed (duraga)[23] and could not tell anything specific about their branch. The ideas of pariah about this group are inconsistent and contradictory. Some of the informants held that *musalli* and *shuya* do not belong to the pariah group and they probably learnt the pariah dialect from the members of the shahi-khel group.[24] The author also heard that the group *shuya*-migrated from Multan and they spoke in a dialect different from that of the pariah.[25]

At present, differences between the different branches of the various groups of pariah are gradually vanishing but not in the distant past which branch of pariah group they belonged to, played not a small role. Even today there is a concept, though fairly inconsistent that one branch was higher and the other was lower. For example, for marriage young men belonging to *kalu* or *juni* branches are preferred. On the other hand young men from *kalu* or *juni* branch do not consider girls from *magar* or *musalli* as their socially equals. However, mixed marriages between different groups of pariah are not rare. However some informants insisted that men belonging to *kalu* branch insist on marrying girls belonging either to *kalu* or *juni* branches. However I have definite information that a *kalu* young man married a girl from the musalli branch. There are instances when *kalu* girls married juni young men and juni girls married *kalu* young men. It appears that *bisiyan* do not enter into marriage alliances with *kalu* (most probably not with the group shahi-khel).

As regards marriage with the representatives of other groups of people, pariah once in a while marry Tajik or Uzbek girls but as a rule they marry their girls only with pariah.[26] The motive is to keep their breed pure 'ustuxân-i-ma safed' *i.e.* literally to 'keep our bone pure and white'.[27] The pariah never enter into marriage relations with Central Asian gypsies (*jugi*) and Central Asian Jews (*juhud, jovut*).

Children born out of mixed marriage are called *duraga*. In the event of the death of elder brother, the younger brother can marry the widow. But when the younger brother dies, the elder brother is not entitled to marry the widow.[28]

As a mark of the identification of the group, the representatives called themselves 'paria'.[29] For them the dialect to be used is Indo-Aryan : *beta tu russi gal na-kar, tu paryasazi gal kar* "Son you do not speak in Russian, you talk in the language of pariah".

As a mark of self-identification, the term "shahi-khel" may also be used (sometimes as a synonym of the 'term pariah)[30]—mentioned above as a subsection of lagmani (laghmoni).

The local population is not aware of these terms and usually calls the members of the group by the common name "afagno" or "afgany".[31] Sometimes the terms used are "*Afgono-yi siyorul (siyopust)*—"dark-faced (dark-skinned Afghans)",[32] or '*afgono-yi nosfurus (nospurus)*—"afgany-sellers of *nas* [tobacco which is used as snuff-trans]".[33] Pariah themselves use the word "afghono" in the sense of describing themselves as "immigrants from Afghanistan". But they clearly distinguish themselves from Pashto or Patani-speaking Afghans and also clearly know the difference between Pashto[34] and their Indo-Aryan dialect.[35]

Among other terms used to denote the pariah, the most interesting are "changar", universally used term sheh-momadi,[36] representatives of the group '*sogutarosh* '[37], *jugi*[38] used for individuals coming from

Afghanistan[39] and Peshawar.[40] The pariah recognise the term "Changar" used by sheh-momadi to denote a group of pariah and are inclined to treat it as a synonymous term for pariah.[41] According to one of the informants from the region of Hissar, "We call ourselves pariah (parya); sheh-momadi call us 'Changar' and our language Changari."

The term "Changar" may point to the relationship of the group under study with the Punjabi tribe (or caste), described under this term in literature. According to G.V. Leitner [38][42] "One of the settlements of Changar exists in Lahore where they live in huts in a compact group. The following places are also recounted by Changars as places where their compatriots live: Ludhiana, Amritsar, Ferozpur, Jallandhar, Peshawar and 'a stage beyond Peshawar'. According to them there were no Changars in Delhi and Rawalpindi and they had never heard of Sindh. The Changars of Lahore affirm that they had come here from Darap (Dagar in Sialkot region[43]) and their ancestors are immigrants from Kashmir and the hills of Pathan. Members of other tribes use the form 'Changar' for them which means according to Leitner, "winnower of grains" (from the Hindi word Chhanna—sifting). The members of this group are engaged in winnowing wheat.[44] It should be noted that among eleven subdivisions or castes of the group of Changar mentioned by Leitner, five coincide with the names of the branches of the pariah; *Kale, Maghare, Jiteyan, Basian Jenu* (in the group of Pariah these are similar to *kalu, magara, jitiyan, bisiyan, juni*). Leitner observes that Changar described by him do not take up black-smithy, fortune-telling, thieving and are not professional musicians and there are no reasons to connect them with the wandering tribes of India.[45] Other factors showing connections of the group under study with the Changar of the Punjab are their feeling, as mentioned earlier, that their ancestors were the disciples of Sheikh Shamsi Tabrizi. There are indications that the Changars of the Punjab were converted to Islam by Shamsi Tabrizi of Multan. *The Dictionary of Tribes and Castes of Punjab and North-West Frontier Province* says, "Changar fem-i, -iani, -ni (Changar in multani)—pariah (outcastes), probably of local origin, are found in great numbers in (Gujarat), Amritsar,

Lahore, Ferozpur, Faridkot but especially in Sialkot. They report that their fore-fathers came from the Jammu hills. In the beginning they were a wandering tribe which roams in search of work and settles down on the outskirts of big towns in colonies. They take up any work but are usually employed in agriculture, especially as reaper. Women are hired for cleaning the grains...All are Muslims...according to them were converted by Shamsi Tabrizi of Multan... They are extremely hard-working and completely free from crime. They have their own dialect..." [42, II, 153]. Unfortunately the present author does not have any example of the dialect of the Changars of the Punjab which could be used for comparison with the dialect of the Central Asian pariah.[46] Nevertheless, the description given above enables us to hypothesize that the Central Asian group of pariah is one of the branches of Changars described in Indian literature at the end of the nineteenth and beginning of the twentieth century as living in various parts of North-Western India.

Some of the terms denoting the various branches of the group of pariah under study are often met in the list of castes and tribes of India. For example, among the "agricultural clan of Jats" Kallu is mentioned in reports prepared at the end of the last century as living in Amritsar, Montgomeri and Shahpur. A similar clan under the name Kalo was reported living in Amritsar and Multan. As *Kalo* their presence was reported in Shahpur and Montgomeri. It is also mentioned that clans *Kallu* and *Kals* were Muslims in Montgomeri [42, II, 441][47] One of the most knowledgeable ethnographers of Afghanistan in the last century, Bellew repeatedly refers to patrimonial sections under the name *Kalu* among different tribes and tribal combinations in Afghanistan [37, 16-17, 24-25, 45, 79, 92, 114-16, 117-19 and others).[48] The genetic term *Kalu* probably originates from the Hindi term *kala*, 'black'.[49]

As regards the different branches of pariah, *juni, magar, jitan,* it should be mentioned that among the 'agricultural Jat clan' *Junhi* is found in Montgomeri [42, II, 416] and clans Mahárá, Máhara and Jhotan in Multan [42, III, 46; II, 387, 416].[50]

The use of the terms 'shahi-khel' and 'mussali' is confusing and indefinite. These terms are used in different regions for different ethnic groups of people. *The Dictionary of Tribes and Castes in the Punjab and North-Western Frontier Provinces* informs us, "Musalli— (the Muhammadan Chuhra) of western Punjab. This term is usually used west of Lahore as synonym for the term 'Kutani'; however, the term 'musalli' is chiefly used in the north-west and 'kutani' in the south-west. Since the newly converted Chuhra continues to eat carion and carries excreta, he is called chuhra. Only when he gives up these habits he is known as musalli. In the frontier cities musalli carries excreta and on the borders of Peshawar he often serves as a grave-digger or sweeper and is called "Shahikhel" [42, III 138]. In other places "Shahikhel—a sweeper" or grave-digger (also called musalli)—Peshawar. In Chah Hazara and along the Indus river—he is a Gypsy, who earns a living by making mats, baskets from cane and other wicker-work" [42, III, 399].[51]

Most of the pariah are inclined to distinguish *musalli* from their group. In any case they distinguish it from the subgroup *shahi-khel* (see above). According to them and according to the members of *Kabol* (*Sheh-momadi*) and other migrants from Afghanistan, *musallis* in Afghanistan are considered of low origin; they stand below Changars (pariah). Another informant (a member of immigrant group from Peshawar), however held that *musalli* was a common term which covers all branches and subgroups and names such as 'Chashgarark' and 'Changar'.[52]

According to him, *musalli*—is nothing but like 'Indian jugi' which in India is called '*Curi*'[53] and which performs there all the dirty work from sweeping the streets to carrying excreta. After conversion to Islam, a significant portion of *musalli* got the opportunity to change their family profession ordained by birth for the outcaste or *chuhra* in the Indian society. They took up work especially in agriculture, generally as manual labourers.

About their social position and their profession by birth among the Afghan tribes, we should see the following verse by the Afghan leader and poet Khushalkhan Khattak (XVII Cent.).

> ma Khushal vai, ma Khatak vai
> ma khani vai
> cac[54] pe las vai, masalli vai,
> kho dzvani vai

"If I were not Khushal, I were not Khattar, I were not Khan; let in my hands be broom, I was a *musalli* but let me be only young"[55].

References to the caste of *musalli* among the Jats living in the western Punjab and speaking a dialect from the Lahanda group, are found in literature. According to the Indian Census Report of 1931, more than 30% *musallis* were engaged in agriculture [7, 231].

Similarly the occasional use of the term 'Chachgarak' (cacgarak, cásgarak), with regard to a group of pariah is also confusing. In the opinion of the native inhabitants of the area, this term is associated with a small immigrant ethnic group. Members of the group sheh-*momadi* use the term '*chachgarak*' with regard to pariah.[56] At the same time this group [the pariah] use the same term for sheh-momadi and point out that '*chachgarark* is a term of abuse' (*ta'na*).[57] The term '*Chachgarak*' seems to come from the word '*chach*'—an instrument for winnowing grains (see above notes) and in Afghanistan means a hired agricultural labour[58] or may be the manufacturer of the instrument.[59]

In Hissar *jugi* is the term used for describing members of the group of pariah. The other terms are *haltuk* and *lum*. The first of them arises probably from the same stock as the subgroup kals (see above), from ancient—Indian *kala* (black, dark)' (-tuk-is a characteristic suffix for the the argoti-speech of *jugi*). The second term is interesting; it is from the ancient Indian term *domba* "person belonging to the lowest caste, professional musicians"[60] [43].

Pariah are not the only ethnic group who migrated to Central Asia via the territory of Afghanistan. Natural geographic conditions and historical and cultural bonds between the left and right banks of the Oxus river facilitated commercial and cultural exchanges between the two areas and made migration of groups of people from both the areas easy. In course of such migration from the left bank of the

Oxus river many ethnic groups came to Central Asia either because of necessity or oppression or due to other circumstances. One such group is known under the name 'Baluj' speaking an Indo-Aryan dialect, It lived in the 70s of the last century in Farghana and Tashkent and was described by the Russian naturalist A.I. Vilkins [5, 436-461]. According to A.I. Vilkins, emigration of a small group 'baluj' from the basin of the Indus river and Baluchistan to Central Asia continued in the 70s of the nineteent century and their route lay through the territories of Afghanistan.

A.I. Vilkins brings out some interesting facts regarding the ethnography and anthropology of the above-mentioned group in his article. He also lists some words under the heading "Some words of Beluji (tribe of Jats?)". This is our only material on the language of Baluj. One could have hoped that the language of these groups, (different from the Central Asians) "should be closely related to each other. But this view was not upheld either ethnographically or linguistically. As distinguished from 'Baluj' and majority of small immigrant groups from Afghanistan to Central Asia (*sheh-momadi*, *chistoni, jugi*)[62], the pariah are from time immemorial agriculturists.

As regards their language, despite all limitations, when the material on the speech of 'baluj' is put against the dialect of pariah—we are able to find important lexical and historical-phonetic differences between the two Indo-Aryan dialects [12,13-16]. This is only the second time that in academic circles, Indian dialects from Central Asia have received attention.

It is possible that the migrants from India were small ethnic groups which moved from Afghanistan to Hissar valley and the adjoining areas and were taken note of by travellers and researchers from the last three decades of the nineteenth century onwards. One of the first observers of this type was G. Bonvalo, who during his travels in 1880s in Central Asia noted the presence of a small settlement (not more than 100 persons) in Hissar of emigrants from Afghanistan. The local population called them 'Kabuliwala' or "Multon". According to Bonvalo they came here around twenty-five years before his arrival (*i.e.* around mid-Nineteenth Century) and for some time led a wandering life like the Gypsies. After some time they settled down in Hissar, cut a canal and began cultivating rice and water-melon. The 'kabuli' of Hissar built mud-houses but at the same time lived in huts built of canes. Externally they looked like Afghans but the local population called them Gypsies [32, 222-224].

Somewhat later S.D. Maslovskii and M.S. Andreev refer to the presence of a group of Afghan immigrants in the Hissar valley and the adjacent areas. In his essay "Tajiks of the Hill—Remains of Original Inhabitants of Turkistan" based on personal observation in eastern Bukhara," Maslovskii spoke of 'wandering tribes', 'long-headed Afghans' with negroid features' [24,113]. In the same article, the author speaks of 'nomadic Afghan tribes, gypsies' whom he saw in Hissar. Their skin was coffee-coloured, cap, curly hair, low fore-head, small but wide and flattened nose, fleshy, fat, spongy, twisted lips and protruding ears" and were dolichocephalic [8, 31-32]. During an ethnographic trip to the Samarkand region in 1921, M. S. Andreev also heard of "augan [afghan?]-people" moving about and showing performances of monkeys and bears and speaking "amongst themselves in a dialect which the outsiders could not understand". However, according to Andreev, on this expedition they could not meet anyone belonging to this group and could not find whether their language was Pashto or "any of the dialects of the gypsies" [1,126].[63]

Unfortunately total lack of information about the language of this group does not give us an opportunity to compare it with the language of the pariah.

Similarly the information about Indian languages being spoken in Afghanistan is meagre. There is comparatively a detailed description of Pasai [40] and other Dardi languages [See 28]. However, these languages and dialects are related to completely different branches of Indo-Aryan languages as compared to the language of the pariah. In the first article relating to the group under study (1956) it was concluded that the language of the pariah belonged to the Central group of Indo-Aryan languages (Grierson's classification).[64] New data discovered during the study of texts and compilation of dictionaries permit us to confirm the above conclusion about the place occupied by the dialect under study in the circle of Indo-Aryan languages and dialects and its place therein. Many similarities connect the dialect of the pariah with different languages of central and north-western part of the Indian subcontinent. There is similarity of the pariah language in terms of phonetics and grammar with similar features of western Hindi, Punjabi, Lehanda, Rajasthani, Gujarati and other languages but taken as a whole the pariah language is not similar to any one of them. This gives the basis to consider the pariah language as an independent dialect of the central group of Indo-Aryan languages[66], which has some specific features of its own and which are not inherent in the other Indo-Aryan dialects.[67]

What language of the Indic group found on the territory of Afghanistan can be even hypothetically akin to the language of the group under study. As has been shown earlier, the Pashai and other Dardic languages belong to an entirely different group of Indo-Aryan languages. On the Afghan territory Indian migrants speak Punjabi, Lehnda, Sindhi, but these are (as in the literature of Central Asia before the November 1917 revolution) traders and moneylenders, who lived in the centre of cities. People speaking Hindustani along with Persian were observed long ago in the eastern part of the valley of Jalalabad [see 23, 628, note 49], Lehanda in Kohdama [north of Kabul]. Morgensterne [41, 5] and other authors observed this [30, 56][68]. Indians of eastern Afghanistan known as "Hindgi (Hindki)" and engaged in agriculture and are similar to Jats, as we learn from *Encyclopaedia Islam* [35, 155]. In this connection the statement of G. Morgensterne deserves attention, "Also Doms and Jatts are said to possess languages of their own" [41.6 note]. Recent surveys of Afghanistan reveal that Punjabi language was spoken in Gazni, Gardez, Kohdaman, Jalalabad [26,70].

As has been stated earlier the most apt comparison of pariah of Hissar Valley is with Changars of the Punjab as shown by Leitner. However, the final conclusion as to with which Indic language group and dialect, the pariah are associated can be reached only after we get authentic material on the language and ethnography of Indic language speakers of North-Western India and Afghanistan.

LITERATURE CONSULTED

1. Andreyev, M.C., "Nekotoriye rezultaty ethnographicheskoi ekspeditsii v Samarkandskoi oblasti v 1921 g." in *Izvestiya Turkestanskogo otdela Russkogo geograficheskogo obschestva*, XVII, 1924.

2. Idem, *Po ethnologii Aghanistana, Dolina Panjshir,* Tashkent, 1927.

3. *Afganskiye skazki* translated from Afghan, Moscow, 1965.

4. Beskrovnyi, M., Krasnodembskii, V.E., *Urdu-russkii slovar,* M., 1951.

5. Vilkins, A.I., "Sredneaziatskaya bogema" in *Antropologicheskay vystavka 1879 g.* T. III, Ch. I, vyp.4,M. 1882; *Izvestiya imp.obshchestva lyubitelei estesto-znaniya, antropologii i etnografil pri imp. Moskovskom universitete*, T. XXXV. ch. I, vyp.4.

6. Zograf, G.A., *Indii, Pakistana, Teseilona i Nepala*, M.,1960.

7. Kudryavtsev, M.K., "Musulmanskiye kasty" in *Kasty v Indii,* M., 1965.

8. Maslovskii, S.D.,"Galcha (pervobytnoye naseleniya Turkestana)" in *Russkii antropologicheskii zhurnal*, 1901, No.2.

9. Miller, V.V., *Persidsko-russkii slovar,* M., 1950.

10. Mukhammed Ali, *Afganistan, Novyi putevodeitel,* M, 1957.

11. *Narody Aziil I Afriki,* 1962, No. 4.

12. Oranskii I.M., "Dva indoariiskikh dialekta iz Srednei Azii" in *Indiiskay i iranskay filologiya*, M, 1964.

13. Idem "Indiiskii dialekt gruppy parya (gissarskay dolina)" in *Materialy i issledovaniya*, vyp. I, Teksty (folkor), M., 1963 (XXVI Mezhdunarodnoi kongress vostokovedov. Materialy delegatsii SSSR).

14. Idem, *Indoiranskiye dialekty Gissarskoi doliny (Indiiskii dialekt parya govory i argo Tajikoyazhichnikh etnograficheskikh grupp).* Materialy i issledovaniya. Avtoref. dokt. diss., Leningrad, 1967.

15. Idem, "Legenda o sheikhe Shamsi Tabrizi" in *Ellinisticheskii Blizhnii Vostok, Vizantiya i Iran*, M. 1967.

16. Idem, "Nauchnaya komandirobka v doliny Gissara i Sarkhan-Darya" in *Sovetskaya Etnorgrafiya*, 1966, No. 4.

17. Idem, "Novyye svedeniya o sekretnikh yazykakh Srednei Azii (I). etnograficheskaya gruppa "kabol" v Kulbe i yee argo" in *KCINA* XL, Yzykoznaniye, M, 1961.

18. Idem, "Novyye svedeniya o sekretnykh yzykakh (argo) Srednei Azii (II).Materialy dlya izucheniya argo etnograficheskoi gruppy jugi (Gissarskaya dolina" in Iranskaya filologiya. *Trudy nauchnoi konferentsii po iranskoi filologi* (24-27 yanvarya 1962g.), LGU, 1964.

19. Idem, "Predvaritelnoye soobshcheniya ob obnaruzhennom v srednei Azil indiiskom dialekte "in *Sovetskoye Vostokoyedeniye*, 1956, No.4

20. Pikulin, M.G., *Afganistan,* Tashkent, 1956.

21. Polyak, A. A., *Fizicheskaya geografia Afganistana,* M. 1953.

22. Rastorgyeva V.C., *Ocherki po Tajikskoi dialekktlogii.* vyp. 5, 1963.

23. Ritter K., *Zemlevedeniye. Geografiya stran Azii, nakhodyshchikhsya v nepospresdstvennykh snosheniyakh s Rossiyei. Kabulistan i Kafiristan. Perevel s prisovokupleniyem kriticheskikh primechanii i dopolnil po istochnikam...* V. V. Grigoryev, SPB., 1867.

24. *Russkii antropologicheskii zhurnal,* 1900, No. 4

25. *Skazki i stikhi Afganistana,* per. s afgan., M. 1958.

26. *Sovremmennyi Afganistan, Spravochnik,* M. 1960.

27. Sukhareva, O.A., "Svadevnye obryady tajikov g. Smarkanda i nekotorykh drugykh raionov Srednei Azii", in *Sovietskaya Antropologia*, collection of articles, III, M.-L., 1940.

28. Edelman D., *Dardskiye yaziki*, M., 1965.

29. Abdu-ul-Ghafur Farhadi, *Le persan parle en Afganistan,* Paris, 1955.

30. *Afghanistan,* Dona N. Wilber (ed), 1956.

31. Bellew, H. W., *An Inquiry into the Ethnography of Afghanistan,* London, 1891.

32. Bonvalot, G., *Through the Heart of Asia,* Vol. 1, London, 1889.

33. *The Encyclopaedia of Islam,* vol. I, London-Leyden, 1913.

34. Hobson-Jobson, *A Glossary of Coloquial Anglo-Indian Words and Phrases, and of Kinderd Terms* by Col. Henry Yule and A.C. Burnell, London, 1903.

35. *The Imperial Gazetteer of India,* vol. XXII, Oxford, 1908.

36. Ivanow N., "The Sect of Imam Shah in Gujarat", in *Journal of the Bombay Branch of Royal Asiatic Society*, N.S., 1936, Vol. XII.

37. Leitner G.W., *Appendix to Changars and linguistic fragments,* Lahore, 1882.

38. Idem, *A Sketch of the Changars and of Their Dialect,* Lahore, 1880.

39. *Linguistic Survey of India,* XI, Calcutta, 1922.

40. Morgenstierne, G., *Indo-Iranian Frontier Languages,* Vol. III. *The Pashai Language, 1. Grammar,* Oslo, 1967; 2. Texts, Oslo, 1944; 3. Vocabulary, Oslo,1956.

41. Idem, *Report of a Linguistic Mission to Afghanistan.* Oslo, 1926.

42. Rose H.A., *Glossary of the Tribes and Castes of the Punjab and the North-West Frontier Province Based on the Census Report for the Punjab, 1883 and the Census Report for the Punjab. 1982.* Lahore, Vol. I, 1919, Vol. II, 1911, vol. III, 1914.

43. Turner, R.L., *A Comparative Dictionary of the Indo-Aryan Languages,* London, 1966.

44. Wolf, S.A., *Grosses Worterbuch der Zigeunersprache* (romani tsiw), Mannheim, 1960.

REFERENCES

1. As per the administrative division of Afghanistan at the end of 1952, the Lagman Valley was a part of the Lagman region consisting of the western section of the Eastern Provinces (Jalalabad). The centre of the region is village Tirgeri (spelled by different authors and in different maps as Tigri, Tigir, Tagir, etc.), situated at the junction of rivers Alingar and Alisheng. See the map attached to the annual *Kabul for the year 1952/1953* and reproduced by M.G. Pikullin [20, between pages 66 and 68], [20, 65 Table 2] and [21, p.110]. Usually the term Lagman refers to the territory situated in the middle and lower reaches of Alisheng and Alingar. However under this term in our sources and in travel accounts often part of the Kabul valley beginning from the "mouth of Lagman valley to Jalalabad including its suburbs and the neighbouring valley is meant". See also [10,70,103-105].

2. By the way some of the members of this group affirmed that their forefathers were migrants from Balkh and Talikan.

3. On divisions among the group of pariah see below, p. 151.

4. M.C. Andreyev wrote of a dialect "of a specific philological group" in village "Bulyagain east of Gulbahar". The deceased scholar hoped to publish some examples of this at a later period [2,3 note]. However, he did not do it. According to information provided by the widow A.K. Pisarich, she failed to discover this in the archives of M.C. Andreyev. Probably Andreyev had met in this area people speaking Pashai. See [40,1,6,16 and ff.].

5. Hazdanahar lierally means "eighteen canals". My informers told me that it is situated somewhere in the region of Balkh.

6. Gilband is referred to in one of the songs.

7. Sahi-khel Shams-i-Tabrizi (Field notes in 1961 in Hissar region). About the term shahi-khel, see below p. 148.

8. As per the words of Sheh-momadi, šaikh-i-Tabriz pir-i Cangaro (pariah) "Sheikh Tabrizi-pir Changarar" [Field notes in Hissar region, 1961]. Pir (Tajik) means spiritual master or spiritual head. About the term 'changar' see below, p. 152. About the group 'kabol' [Shekh momadi] see [17, 62 and ff. 16,127 and ff.].

9. Field Notes, Hissar Valley, 1961.

10. For the text and translation of this legend, see [15].

11. See [42, 1, 546]. There and further on there are more references. V.A. Ivanov informs me that the keepers of the grave of Shams Tabrizi identify him with the famous spiritual teacher Jalal-al Din Rumi. See [36, 29 and ff.]. *Ibid* (including p. 49). Photograph of the grave on p. 49. From the list of the works of Ivanov, it appears that he has published an article on this Multani Sheikh. However, the present author was unable to lay his hands upon this article.

12. It is not clear if he was the spiritual teacher only for the pariah or other groups of population as well.

13. Many scholars writing about Afghanistan and travellers to the country speak of Mazar-i Sharif as a holy place and a centre of pilgrimage. See [20,231]. See also new guide [10, 121-122]. *Ibid*. At the end of the book there is a photograph of the tomb.

14. One of the songs has the story of the girl who intended to go on a pilgrimage to Mazar-i Sharif so that she could marry her lover. The song about the pilgrimage to Mazar-i Sharif is very interesting as it refers to the killing of animals for feeding the pilgrims. These animals had been offered at the tomb.

15. See [13, Texts No. IV, VIII, IX, XIV, and others]. The same is the case with the anecdotes relating to the cycle of Afandi [No. X-XII].

16. See for example the description of the pir in one of the stories [13, No. 18].

17. See [3,93 and ff.], same translation in [25, 88 and ff.].

18. By including the *beits* in the story, the Afghan heroes pour out their feelings to one another. In Afghan language the word is para, literally meaning 'cry or exclamation'. [the word is from Arabic-Persian].My informant who narrated this story called them *fajra* [Tajik *faryod* 'cry, exclamation'].

19. Researchers at the Institute of Languages and Literature, AN Tajikistan SSR familiar with the musical tradition of Tajik and Uzbek folklores, after hearing the tapes of the songs, told me that they had not heard of these melodies before.

20. Field Notes, 1961 and 1964 [Hissar and Regar regions of Tajikistan SSR].

21. Thus in the settlement Novabad [local name Kara-Bolo in the Leninskii, region], the members of the subdivision bisiyan live in close neighbourhood of the group Kabol. There are indications that the members of the (or at least some among them) Bisiyans know the secret language (argo) of the *Kabols* [Field Notes, 1961, Hissar and Sahrineu regions of the Tajikistan SSR].

22. Some families of this subdivision also live in the Regar region of Tajikstan SSR and Denau region of Uzbekistan SSR. [Oral evidence].

23. One of them Nur Ali affirmed that his father comes from Khanabad (northern Afghanistan) and his mother from Kangurt (near Kulyab region of Tajikstan SSR). After the death of his father, his mother was married again to a member of the group of pariah. In this family as a child, Nur Ali learnt the language.

24. Field Notes, 1961 [Hissar region].

25. The example was given that *Shuya* spoke *'asi'* for 'come here' *'jasi'* for 'go there or get out' (corresponding to *'aja'* and *'ja'* in the dialect of the pariah). In dialect *kabuli* (and almost everywhere in Afghanistan) the word "*shuya*" means shiite (*šujá*) See for example, [29, 15]. Is the name of the above group not connected with the name of the above subdivision? Compare this with the fact that the followers of Sheikh Shamsi Tabrizi in Multan were followers of the Shiite section of Islam.

26. The group *"Kabol"* (Shekh-momadi),migrant from Afghanistan is the only exception. It is well known that in some cases, members of this group gave in marriage their daughters to *pashtuns (Kandahori)*.

27. The custom of daughter being given in marriage to the members of the same group is well known among many groups of population in Central Asia (alkhoja and seids) and in Afghanistan due to a variety of reasons. See [2,13]. According to the information given by N.A. Kislayakov, such a tendency generally characterises small ethnic groups in Central Asia.

28. Compare the same tendency among the Tajiks, at least in several regions of Central Asia [27, 123].

29. About the term "pariah" as the name of the lowest caste among the Hindus see [34, 678].

    One of the important characteristics of the dialect of the pariah which unites it with the dialects of the Punjab is the correspondence of the beginning 'p' with the beginner 'bh' of Hindustani. In connection with this phonetic transformation one's attention is drawn to the name of the clans of agriculturists Jats, Bhar, Bharah, in Multan, Bharyar in Amritsar; the name Bharmi is found all over Punjab and the North-Western provinces. They are Muslims and they include members of different ethnic and caste groups [42, II, 84-86, 90].

30. Field Notes, 1961 [Hissar region].

31. As has been noted [11,243 and ff.] the term "Afghon" is used by the locals to denote all migrants from Afghanistan. It does not in any way denote the linguistic or ethnic belonging of a person or group. This undifferentiated use of the term "Afghon" has unfortunately become popular in literature as well.

32. The dark colour of the skin is considered to be the characteristic of the group under study by the local population.

33. *Nas* (Tajik *nos*) or snuff—a local preparation of tobacco for sniffing. Many pariah are engaged in preparing snuff for sale among the local population. The local population considers this activity of the pariah as their specialised craft.

34. The term *patan* usually used for Afghans of the North-Western Frontier Provinces of India and its adjoining regions may be an evidence of the acquaintance or the pariah with groups of Afghan tribes of Eastern Afghanistan.

35. The last according to reasons cited above is also sometimes known as "Afghani" (*lafz-i afghoni, zabon-i afghoni*).

36. Field Notes, 1957 [Kulyab], 1961,and 1964 [Hissar region].

37. Field Notes, 1959 [village Khankin Hissar region]. About the group *sogutorosh* see [16,128].

38. Field Notes, 1959 [Hissar and Koktas region of the Tajikstan SSR]. For *jugi* of Hissar see [18,62 and ff.].

39. Field Notes, 1958 [village Khanak in Hissar region] and 1961 [village Tula of Hissar region].

40. Field Notes, 1959 [Hilly Khanak, Hissar region].

41. Field Notes, 1956, 1961, 1964 [Hissar region]. 1958 [Regar region].

42. I have not been able to get another work [37] of this author.

43. A group of labourers, known as Changar was found among the lowest castes in the region of Sialkot. They numbered 6000.

44. V.V. Kushev during his visit to Afghanistan noted Changars, distinguished by their dark skin and working as winnowers of grains in Lagman. An Afghan from Tigri, as communicated by V.V. Kushev, also spoke of them.

45. It is not excluded that in India there were and there are tribes, including nomadic tribes, known as Changar. E. Trumpp refers to Changars, roaming along the banks of the rivers of the Punjab and speaking Sindhi. They probably do not have anything common with the Changars described by Leitner. Probably the later do not recognise them as co-tribesmen. N. A. Dvoryankov, who collected information regarding the use of certain ethnic terms at my request during his stay in Afghanistan informed me (letter from Kabul dated 28/1/1963) that an ethnic group marked by dark skin and a nomadic way of life and called *cangar* or *cangari* is found in the regions of Jalalabad and Laghman. The plural of *cangar* is *cangariyan*. They call their language *linko* or *hinduko* (*i.e.* the same term by which the languages of Jats, Gujars and sometimes of Hindusthanis in Afghanistan is described).

46. Lexicographical material and phrases used in the dialect of Changars as presented in the above-mentioned work of Leitner. He gives words and phrases from one of the artificial languages of India (argo) and cannot serve this aim. see [13, 182 and ff.].

47. In the same work some more tribes and clans are mentioned [Kalru in Multan], names which include the element "kal". They may be just variations of the same ethnic term.

48. The problem whether these groups have any direct relationship with the subdivision "kalo" in the Hissar Valley still remains open.

49. Compare with "kalo" "dark", black" in the dialect of the pariah. Also compare its use in the dialects of European gypsies where the word "kalo" has two meanings—(a) black and (b) gypsy. See [44].

50. According to information collected by V.V. Kushev at my request, *jutan* is a tribe in India, having specific dress and languages. The members of this group are often hired for heavy work, such as porters on the Indian railways, and such jobs.

51. It follows that in this connection we should keep in mind all the attending circumstances and the vagueness of the term Gypsy, which is used by western authors to denote all the nomadic and roaming tribes of India and its adjoining countries. See, for example [39, I and ff.].

52. Field Notes, 1958 [Hilly Khanka]. According to information collected in Afghanistan by N.A. Dvoryanikov and V.V. Dushev the term *'musalli'* is considered identical with the term *'Changar'* in Jalalabad; in other regions of Afghanistan— with the term *'chachgark'* in the Kunar. Information received from N.A. Dvoryanik. This group speaks Persian (in Jalalabad) or Persian and Pashto and does not have any specific language of its own.

53. Compare with the Hindi word 'cuhra' the caste of sweepers in the Punjab and North-Western India [4,837]. In the dialect of *kabuli* the term *'musali'* has been invested with the meaning "collector of garbage, sweeper, yard-keeper' [9, 864].

54. Chach—lash made from the mat of cane with the help of which grain is winnowed [Field Notes, 1961, Hissar region]. Compare it with *cac* in the dialect of *kabuli* which means 'tray for cleaning grains during thrashing' [9.262]. In the *Shahristan* dialect of Tajik languages *'cos'* means sieve with rouned holes for winnowing grains [22, 217]

55. Information contained in the letter sent by N.A. Dvoryanikov from Kabul dated 28/1/1963.

56. Field Notes, 1961 [Hissar and Leninski region]. It is strange that the term *'chachgarak'* was used also by the representatives for the subdivision *'bisiyan'* with regard to subdivision *'dalu'* even though they and their neighbours *'sheh-momadi'* hold that the subdivision 'bisiyan' does not belong to the group 'chachgarak'.

57. Field Notes, 1956 and 1961 [Hissar region].

58. Field Notes, 1961 [Hissar region].

59. According to information received from N.A. Dvoryanikov, this term in Afghanistan is understood in the following manner. The '*Chachgarak*' is also known as '*musali*'. Compare this with the reference to '*chache*' as an attribute of '*musali*' in the poem of Khushal Khan cited above.

60. From this base springs 'rom' 'husband, man' in the dialect of European gypsies. The beginning with '1' is witnessed only in the dialect of Armenian gypsies (bosha)—Iom.

61. According to "baluji", the Indians called them "paniraj" (5,440). Do we not see here the misprint of 'paniraj' in place of 'pakiraj'? According to one of my informants from Samarkand, Kh.Kh. Nazarov, the natives of Samarkand interested in the ethnography of their group in Samarkand region, Bukhara and Shahrsabz to this day find 150 families of Indian gypsies known as 'pokoroch/pakoroch' [letter dated 25.III.1965]. Kh.Kh. Nazarov informs me that the language of this group, which in the past was engaged in the handicraft of jewellery, differs considerably from the language of 'local gypsies'. If the hypothesis about the misprint is confirmed then 'paniraji' of Vilkins are direct ancestors of modern 'pokoroch' (the interchange of i into a in the protonic syllable and j into c at at the end of the word is easily explained).

62. About these groups see [16, 127-129].

63. The local population applied the term 'Afghan' or 'Indian/Hindustani' 'also to' Balujs'. A. I. Vilkins notes that among their occupations was showing the performances of monkeys and bears (5,440 and ff.). According to information given by N.A. Dvoryanik 'changars' in Jalalabad and Lagman are still engaged in showing the performances of monkeys (letter dated 28/I/1963). However, he notes that the term 'changar' in this place can be used in a very wide manner— to denote any non-Afghan tribe.

64. In this context, we must keep in mind the relative classification arrived at by Grierson. In fact, it should be observed in all the cases which follow [6,20 and ff.].

65. About the absence of a clear linguistic boundary between the dialects of these languages, see [16, 22, 23, 52, 54,58 and others].

66. See the opinion of Morgenstierne, "It is really most surprising and of great interest, to find a comparatively recent offshoot of Indo-Aryan languages in the Hissar valley, and it would be very valuable to investigate if any traces of related dialects could be found among the Jats of

Afghanistan, and other groups of similar types." Letter dated 8/4/1964 sent to the author.

67. An attempt was recently made by the author to give a summary of the specific features of the speech of the pariah by comparing it with the nearest related Indo-Aryan group of languages and dialects [4,21 and ff.].

68. In this context it should be noted that the Indic-speaking population living in Kohdaman is agriculturist (distinct from the population living in Eastern Afghanistan where they are mostly traders or traders in medicinal herbs and bakers).

Bibliography

Archival Sources

National Archives of India, New Delhi

Foreign Department Secret, 25 Nov. 1831, No.3

Foreign Department, Secret A, Nov. 1854, Nos. 1-22

Foreign Department, Secret, Home Branch 1869, 94/96,K.W.Sec. March 1875, Nos. 19-29

Foreign Department, Secret, March 1875, Nos. 19-29. Central Asian Affairs and Appointments of a Permanent Resident in Cashmere

Foreign Department, Secret, August 1876, Nos. 56-57,Newsletter from F.B.

Foreign Department, Secret, 1879, Nos. 829/30A.Correspondence between Kashmir and Trans-Frontier states other than Kabul

Foreign Department, Secret, June 1880, Nos.139-144, No. 143

Foreign Department, Secret, August 1882, No. 351

Foreign Department, Secret, August 1882, Nos. 349-359

Foreign Department, Secret, February, 1882, Nos. 24-32

Foreign Department, Secret, August 1882, No. 351, 349-59

Foreign Department, Secret F, May 1886, Nos. 39-97

Foreign Department, Secret F, Feb. 1886, Nos. 60-70

Foreign Department, Pol. A, Dec. 1864, Nos. 238-240

Foreign Department, Pol. A, Feb. 1865, Nos. 151/154

Foreign Department, Pol. A, June 1866, Nos. 171/173

Foreign Department, Pol. A., K.W., Proceedings, November 1868, Nos.1-4. "Trade with Central Asia, Proposed Negotiations with Russia."

Foreign Department, Pol. A, Proceedings January 1868, No. 89

Foreign Department, Frontier A, Dec. 1887, Nos 1-10

Foreign Department, Pol. B Progs., Nov. 1871, No. 31

Foreign Department, General B. Progs, Jan. 1872, Nos 329/331

Foreign and Political Department, External, Part B, Secret Proceedings, November 1922, Nos. 33-94, p.2

Foreign Department, Pol. Progs., 869, No 65

Foreign Department. Pol.,Despatch to Secretary of State, 24 January 867 No. 19

Telegram P. No. 15733, dated 21 Nov. 1918 from the Viceroy to the Secretary of State, London

Extracts from Thuggie and Dacoity Department, Special Branch, Abstracts of Intelligence, Vol.2 (Calcutta, 4th March 1889) No. 10, Political Movements, Sects, Leaders & Co.

Foreign and Political Deptt., Secret- External Proceedings,August 1920, Nos. 253-256. Report of the Kashgar Mission 1918-1920

Punjab State Archives Travels in Central Asia, M/357/4346/p.23

Archives in the Constituent Countries of the former USSR (not in alphabetical order)

Tsentralnyi Gosudarstvenyi Arkhiv, Uz SSR

F. N-1, op. 32, d.280

F. VI-126, op.1, d. 1132, 11133, 1134

F. VI-d., op. 31, d. 677, L.9-10, 16

F. VI-d., op. 32, d. 280, L.473

F. VI-126, op.1, d. 1133

F. VI-19, op. 1,d. 10738, L.53

F. VI-d. 28889, L. 17

F-1, op. 31, d. 848, L. 13

F-1, op.31, d.677, L. 7, 9-10

F-126, op. 1, d. 93, 96

F-1, op. 29, d. 238, L. 2

F-36, op. 1, d. 1477, L.1,3,5,9, etc.

F-36, op. 1, d. 1287, L. 18

F-36, op. 1, d. 3226,

F-1, op. 22, d. 204 L.10

F-26, op.1, d. 621, L. 209, 283

F-17, op. 11, d. 1663

F-17, op. 11, d. 385, L. 5-9

F-1, op.31, d.677, L. 7,9-10

F-1, op. 34, d.524, L. 81

F-5, op. 1, d. 2655, L. 13

F-1, op.32, d. 213, L. 126

F-1, op. 34, d. 714, L. 1-2

F-136, op.1, d. 1962, L.7

F-136, op.1, d. 3326, L.10

F-136, op.1, d. 3691, L.24

F-46, op.1, d. 361, L.2,13

F-46, op. 1, d. 269, L.77-78

F-471,op.1, d. 10, L.33,44,and following

F-1, op. 32, d. 267, L.441

F-2, op. 2, d. 586, L.1, 2,7,10,13

F-185, op.1, d.132, L.100

F-1, op.32, d.247, L.114

F-1, op.32, d.286, L.330

F-1, op.32, d.248, L.179

F-1, op.32, d.261, L.26

F-185, op.1, d.132, L.100

F-1, op.20, d.3677, L.3

F-1, op.27, d.517, L.5

F-1, op.16, d.208, L.16

F-46, op.1, d.1027, L.245

F-46, op.1, d.269, L.178-79

F-504, op.1, d.3109, L.10

F-504, op.1, d.136, L.213-14

F-504, op.1, d.783, L.75

F-19, op.1, d.26793, L.2

F-18, op.1, d.13168, L.5

F-126, op.1, d.93

F-126, op.1, d.822

F-510, op.1, d.25, L.15

F-510, op.1, d.26, L.1

F-23, op.1, d.239, L.6-7

F-1, op.31, d.282, L.5

F-1, op.31, d.586, L.58

F-1, op.31, d.10001, L.27

F-133, op.1, d.1389, L.7

F-5, op.1, d.2595, L.6,8

F-47, op.1, d.82, L.30

F-47, op.1, d.97, L.3

F-1, op.29, d.1292, L.1

F-1, op.1, d.58,L.1, 6-7

F-40, op.1, d.17, L.8

F-3, op.2, d.35, L.24, 62-63

F-3, op.1, d.359, L.4,6,8

F-3, op.2, d.35, L.108

F.1-473, d.35, L.28

F.1-1, op.6, d.984, L.4

F.1-1, op.6, d.719, L.400

F.1-46, op1, d.361, L.306

F.1-36, op., d.620, 782, 853, 1429, 1516,
 1567, 1570, 1740-1744

F.1-17, op.1, d.3933

F.1-22, op.1, d.45, 2043

F.1- op.11, d.39, L.1-95

F.200, op.263/916a, d.326, L.22

F.1-19, op.1, d.26793, L.2

F.75, op.35, d.2

F.KTGG, op.34, d.25, L.20-22

F.KGGG, op.34, F.462, L.89

AVPR (Arkhiv Vneshnii Politiki Rossii)

F. Konsul v Bombee, d.110, l21

F. Spb. Glav Arkhiv, 11-26, 1811, d4, L.11,12

F. Spb. Glav Arkhiv, 11-3, 1811, d.5, L.12

Sredne-Aziatskii Stol, 1903, No922, L.106-109

F. Spb. Glav. Arkhiv, II-3, 1811, D-5, L-12

F. Spb. Glav Arkhiv, II-26, 1811, d.4, L.11-12

Ts. Glavnyi Voennyi Istoricheskii Arkhiv USSR (Ts GVIA USSR)

F. 400, op.263/916a, d.326, L.22

F. 400, op.261/911, No.111, L.13-14

F. 483, d.95

VUA, F. 483

F. 400, op.261/91, d.51

Tsentralnyi Gosudarstvenyi Arkhiv USSR (Ts G A USSR)

F. 1396, op.2, d.1589, L.181-182

F. 1396, op.2, d.1532, L.9-10

F. 1396, op.2, d.1662, L.234

F. 1396, op.2, d.520, L.9-11, 19

F.400,Aziatsky klast,op.261/911,d.520,L.9-11,19

Glavny Arkhiv (G A)

F-1, P-27, op.43, 1882, d.5, f 330

Leningradskoye Otdeleniya Instuta Narodov Azii (Akademi Nauk, USSR) Ms. Ind.IV, 22

Printed material from Russian archives

Antonova, Goldberg and Lavrentshova (eds.), Russko-Indiiskiye Otnosheniya v XVII V., Moscow, 1958

K.K.Antonova R.V. Ovchinnikov and M.A. Sidorov (compilers and ed.) Russko- Indiiskiye Otnosheniye vXVIII.V, *Moscow,* and 1965

N. Mayev, *Aziatskii Tashkent - Materialy dlya statistiki Turkestanskogo Kraya, Vypuska IV, SPB, 1876*

P.I. Nebolsin, *Ocherki torgovli Rossii so Srednei Azii zapiski Imp. Russkogo geogrficheskogo obshchestva,* Kn. X, 1855

Skobelov, *Obzor Ferganskoi doliny za 1909g., Appendix Obzor Zakaspiiskoi Oblasti za 1890-1896 gg. Vsesoyuznay perepis naseleniya,* 1926, vol. XV, Uzbekskaya SSR

Travel Accounts

M. Albrecht, *Russiche Central asien,* Hamburg, 1896

Bernier, *Travels in the Mogul Empire (Trans. A. Constable),* New Delhi, 1968

L.V.S. Blacker, *On Secret Patrol in High Asia,* London,1922

G. Bonvalot, *Through the Heart of Asia,* Vol. I, London, 1889

A. Burnes, *Travels into Bukhara : Being the Account of a Journey from India to Cabool, Tartary and Persia,* Vol 1, London, 1834

P.T. Etherton, *In the Heart of Asia,* London 1925

Fraser, *Narrative of a Journey to Kharasan in the Years 1821 & 1822,* Delhi, 1984

George Forster, *A Journey from Bengal to England,* Vol. II, Patiala, 1970

Meer Izzut-oolah, *Travels in Central Asia by Meer Izzut-oolah in the Years 1812-13,* Calcutta, 1872

Mohan Lal, *Travel in the Punjab, Afghanistan and Turkistan to Bulkh, Bokhara and Herat and a Visit to Great Britain and Germany,* Calcutta, 1977

Manucci, *Storia do Mogor,* Vol.II (trans. By Irvine), London, 1907

Samuel Purchas, *Purchas His Pilgrimes,* Vol. IV, Glasgow, 1906

E. Schuyler, *Turkistan, Notes of a Journey in Russian Turkistan, Khokand, Bukharas and Kulja,* Vol. 1 and 2, London, 1876

G.T. Vigne, *A Personal Narrative of a Visit to Ghuzni, Kabul, Afghanistan,* New Delhi, 1986

In Russian

A.A. Kuznetsov (ed), *Khozheniye kuptsa Fedeta Kotova v Persiyu,* Moscow, 1958

Shastitko, *Rossiskiye Puteshestvenniki v Indii XIX-nachalo XX v.* Moscow, 1990

N. Khanykov, *Opisanie Bukharskogo Khanstva,* St. Petersburg, 1843

Other Printed Sources

Mountstuart Elphinstone, *An Account of the Kingdom of Cabul,* Vol.II, Karachi

Source Material for a History of Freedom Movement In India, Vol.II

Proceedings of the Russian Geographical Society, Book X, St. Petersburg, 1855

Military Report on Russian Turkistan, General Staff India, 1914

B.V. Miller, *Persidsko-russkii slovar, Moscow,* 1950

Manuscripts

Badruddin Kashmiri, *"Rauzat-ut-Rizwan"*

Persian chronicles translated into English

A Badaoni, *Muntkhabu-t-Tawariakh,* Vol.II, Patna, 1972

Begley and Desai(eds), *The Shah Jahan Name of Inayat Khan,* Delhi, 1990

Abul Fazl, *Ain-I-Akbari,* Vol. II, Delhi, 1989

Jahangir, *The Tuzuk-I-Jahangiri,* Delhi, 1968

Jauhar, *The Tezkerah Al Wakiat,* New Delhi, 1970

Bibliography

Saqui Musta'ad Khan, *Maasir-I-Alamgiri* (trans. into English by Jadunath Sarkar)

I.H. Siddiqui *(tr.)*, *Tarikh-I-Manazil-I-Bukhara*, Srinagar, 1982

Persian Chronicles translated into Russian

Babur, *Babur-name* (Russian translation by S. Salye), Tashkent, 1958

Ghiyasuddin Ali, *Dnevnik pokhoda Timura v Indiyu* (Russian version of "Kitab Roznamai Ghazbat Hindustan Talif al Din Ali bin Jamal al -salam"), Moscow, 1958

Muhammad Kazim, *Pokhodd Nadir Shaha v Indiyu*, Moscow, 1961

Muhammad Yusuf Munshi, *Mukimkhanskaya Istoriya*, Tashkent, 1956

Khoja Samandar Termizi, *Dustur al-Muluk* (trans. into Russian by M.A. Salahkhetdinova), Moscow, 1971

Persian chronicle translated into Uzbek

A. Urinboev, *Abdurrazzok Samarkandii ning Hinduston Safarnomasi*, Tashkent, 1960

Secondary Sources

Books

S.P. Chablani, *Economic Conditions in Sind*, Bombay, 1951

C.H. Ellis, *The Transcaspian Episode*, London, 1963

Peter Hopkirk, *The Great Game*, OUP, New Delhi, 1991

Riazul Islam, *Indo-Persian Relations*, Teharan, 1970

Sir William Jones, *History of Nadirshah*, Vol. I, Delhi, n.d.

N.A. Khalfin, *Politika Rossii v Srednei Azii*, Moscow, 1960

H. Landell, *Russian Central Asia*, London, 1885

G.W. Leitner, *Appendix to Changars and Linguistic Fragments*, Lahore, 1882

Idem, *A Sketch of the Changars and of their Dialect*, Lahore, 1880

R.C. Majumdar, *British Paramountcy and Indian Renaissance*, Vol. I, Bombay,1963

Indra Singh Rawat, *Indian Explorers of the 19th Century*, New Delhi, 1973

G. Moorgensteinerne, *Indo-Iranian Frontier Languages*, Vol. III. the Pashai Language ..I. Grammar, Oslo, 1967; 2. Texts, Oslo, 1944; 3. Vocabulary, Oslo, 1956

Idem, Report of a Linguistic Mission to Afghanistan. Oslo,1926

M.G. Pikulin, *Afghanistan*, Tashkent, 1956

Bisheshwar Prasad, *India's Foreign Policy*, Vol. I,

H. Rawlinson, *England and Russia in the East*, London, 1875

Niels Steensgaard, *The Asian Trade Revolution of the Seventeenth Century*, Chicago, 1974

H.C. Verma, *Medieval Routes to India*, Calcutta, 1978

V. Terway *East India Company and Russia (1800-1857)*, New Delhi, 1977

A. Vambery, *History of Bokhara*, 1873

K.M. Warikoo, *Central Asia and Kashmir*, New Delhi, 1989

Donald N. Wilber (ed.), *Afghanistan*, 1956

French

Abd-ul-Ghafur Farhadi, *Le person parle en Afganistan*, Paris, 1955

Russian

Afganskiye skazki, *translated from Afghan, Moscow, 1965*

M.C. Andreyev, *Po etnologii Afganistana, Dolina Panjsir*, Tashkent, 1927

Mukhamad Ali, *Afganistan, Novyi Putevoditel*, Moscow, 1957

G.A Arendarenko, *Dosugi v Turkestana 1874-1889*, St. Petersburg, 1889

Armenia Pod vlastyu Ahmad Shah Durani

M.A. Babakhodzhaev, *Russko-Afghanskie torgovoekonomicheskiye svyazi*, Tashkent, 1965

V. Bartold, *Istoriya Izycheniya Vostoka v Evrope I v Rossii*, Moscow, 1928

M.K. Gandhi, *Moya zhizn*, Moscow, 1959

D. Edelman, *Dardskiy Yaziki*, M., 1969

Gankovsky, *Imperiya Durrani*, Moscow, 1958

I.I.Geier, *Ves Russkii Turkestana*, Tashkent, 1908

Ya. G. Gulyamov(Chief Editor), *Istoriya Uzbekistan*, Vol. I-III, Tashkent, 1967

Izvestiya imp. Obshchestva lyubitelei estestvo-znaniya, antropologii i etnografii pri imp. Moskovskom universitete, T. XXXV, Ch.I, vyp.4

N. A. Khalfin and P.M. Shaatitko (ed), *Rossiya i India*, Moscow, 1976

N. P. Kolomiitsev, *Chai, mirovaya torgovlia Chaem I vopros o Kazennoi Chainoi monopolii v Rosii*, Moscow, 1916

V. V. Krestovskii, *V Gostiakh u Emira Bukharskogo Khanstvo*, St. Petersburg, 1887

Marx and Engles, *Sochinenya*, T.XVI, Ch. II

A. Vambery, *Puteshestviye po Srednei Azii*, St. Petersburg, 1865

Bibliography

D.P. Krasnovskii (ed), *Vneshnaya Torgovlya Bukhary do voiny*, Tashkent, 1922

R.G. Mukhminova, *Sotsialnaya Differentsiatsiya Naseleniya Gorodov Uzbekistana v XVII vv.*, Tashkent 1985

N.B. Novikova, *Rol Srednei Azii v Russo-Indiiskikh Torgovykh Svyazakh*, Tashkent, 1964

A.A. Polyak, *Fizicheskaya Geografia Afghanistana*, M., 1963

V.C. Rastorgyeva, *Ocherki po Tajikskoi dialektologii*, vyp.5, M.,1963

P.N. Rasul-zade, *Iz Istorii Sredne-Aziatsko-Indiiskikh Svyazei*, Tashkent, 1960

K. Ritter, *Zemlevedeniye stran Azii, nakhodyashchikhsya v neposredstvennykh snosheniyaleh s prisovok upleniyem kriticheskikh primechanii I dopolonii po istochnikam V.V. Grigoryev*, SPB, 1867

Skazki, *I stikhi Afganistana, perevod s afgana*, M, 1958

Yu. Sokolov, *Tashkent, Tashkentsy i Rossiya*, Tashkent,1965

Sovremmenyi Afganistana s spravochnik, M. 1960

G.A. Zograf, *Indii, Pakistana, Tseilona i Nepala*, Moscow, 1960

ARTICLES

A.F. Gubarevich- Radobylskii, "Znachenie Turkestana v torgovle Rossii s sopredel'nymi stranami Azii" in *Materialy dlya izucheniya Khlopokovodstva*, vyp.II, St. Petersburg, 19123

V.F. Novitskii, "Iz Indii v Ferganu" in *Sbornik geograficheskikh, topograficheskikh I statisticheskikh materialov po Azii, Vyp. LXXVI*, St. Petersburg, 1898, pp. 168-69

V.O.Klemm, "Sovremennoe Sostoyanie torgovli v Bukharskom Khanstve", *Sbornik geograficheskikh, topograficheskikh I statisticheskikh materialov po Azii*, vyp. 33, St. Petersburg, 1888

Mohammad Ashraf Wani, "Transfer of Military Technology from Central Asia to India," *The Journal of Central Asian Studies*, No. 1, 1992.

T.A.Lapteva and M.P. Lukichev, "Documents of the USSR State Archives of Ancient Acts Pertaining to the History of Russian- Indian Relations," *Proceedings*, Indian Historical Records Commission, Vol.LII, Srinagar, 1988

A.S. Yukht, " Indiiskaya kolonia v Astrakhani," *Voprosy Istorii*, 1957, No.3,

P.E. Matvievskii, "U roli Orenburga v Russko-Indiiskoi Torgovle v XVIII v." *Istoriya SSSR*, No.3, 1969,

P.E. Matvievskii, "Gens I ego Orenburgakaya Zapisi O russko-indiiskikh svyazyakh v XVIII- pervoi treti XIX veka," *Iz Istorri Yuzhnogo Urala I Za - Urala*, 1966,

O.A. Sukhareva, "Svadevnyeobryadytajikov g. Samarkanda i nekotorykh drugykh raionoy Srednei Azii", *Sovietskaya Antropologia,* collection of statei, III, ML., 1940

A.M. Matto, "Shawl Industry In Kashmir In The Mughal Period", *Proceedings, IHC,* 36th session, Aligarh, 1975,

Idem "Commercial Interaction Between Kashmir & Central Asia", The *Journal of Central Asian Studies,* vol.3, No.1, 1992, pp. 36-39

Dr. Humaira Dasti, "Multan as A Centre of Trade and Commerce During The Mughal Period," *Journal of the Pakistan Historical Society ,* Vol.XXXVIII, July, 1990, part III

Susil Choudhuri, "The 'Silky' World of Bengal Trade," *Proceedings, IHC,* 52nd Session, Delhi, 1992

Surendra Gopal, "Aspects of Indo-Persian trade in the seventeenth century", *Proceedings,* IHC, Varanasi, 1969, pp. 240-46.

B.L. Gupta, " The migration of Traders to Rajasthan in the eighteenth century", *Proceedings,* IHC, Goa, 1988, pp.312-17

N. Ivanow, "The Sect of Imam Shah in Gujarat," *Journal of the Bombay Branch of Royal Asiatic Society,* N.S., 1936, Vol.XII

I. Nizamutdinov, "Maasir-I - Alamgiri-kak istochnik po vneshnopoliticheskim snosheniya Indii", in S.A. Azimzanova and I.M. Khasimov(eds), *India,* Tashkent, 1973

O. Buriyev and A. Kolganov, "Ob Odnom Uchastke Velikogo Shelkogo Puti" G.A. Pugachenkova(ed), *Na Sredne-aziatskikh trasakh velikogo shelkogo puti, Tashkent, 1990*

P.M. Shastitko, "Missiya Mekhti Rafialova k Ranjit Singhu", *Sovetskoye Vostokovedeniye,* 1957, No.4

A.V. Raikov, " Anglo-Indiiskaya Armia natsional'no osvoboditelniya dvizheniye v Indii v 1905-1917 godakh", *Problemy Vostokovedeniya,* No.2, Moscow, 1959

M.C. Andreyev, "Nekotoriye rezultaty etnograficheskoi ekspeditssii v Samarkandskoi oblasti v 1921g." *Izvestia Turkestanskogo otdela Russkogo geograficheskogo obshchestva, XVII, 1924*

M. Andreyeyev, "Nashi tovary na rynke Indii, "*Turkestanskii Sbornik,* T. 458, 1908, p. 149

A Correspondent, "The Revolt in Transcaspia 1918-1919" in *Central Asian Review ,* 1954, Vol.VII, No.2, pp.117-130

G.L. Dmitriyev, "Iz Istorii Indiiskikh kolonii v Srednei Azii" in D.A. Ol'derogge (ed), *Strany I Narody Vostoka, Indiya-Strana I Narody,* Kniga 2, Moscow, 1972

Bibliography

A. Khoshkin, "Samarkand" in *Turkestanskiye Vedmosti,* 1872, No.44

M.K.Kudryavtsev, "Musulmanskiye kasty," *Kasty v Indii,* Moscow, 1965

N.A. Lykoshin, "Pismo iz tuzemnogo Tashkenta", *Turkestanskiye Vedmosti,* 1896, No. 92

S.D. Maslovskii, "Galcha(Pervobytnoye naseleniya Turkestana)", *Russkii Antropologicheskii Zhurnal,* 190, No. 2

W. Malleson, "The Twenty-Six Commissars", *Fortnightly Review,* 1933

W. Malleson, "The British Military Mission to Turkestan 1918-1920", *Journal of the Central Asia Society,* vol.IX, 1922

S.V. Petrov-Baturich, "Vstrecha s plemyannikom Nane- Saiba v Peterburge", *Russkii Vestnik,* 1879, No.6

A.I.Vilkins, "Sredneaziatskay bogema" *Antropologicheskay vystavka 1879 g.* T. III, ch.I, Vyp.4, Moscow, 1882

I.M.Oranskii, "Dva indoariiskikh dialekta iz srednei Azii" *Indiiskaya I iranskaya filologiya,* M. 1964

Idem, "Indiiskii dialekt gruppy parya gissarskay dolina", *Matarialy I issledovaniya,* vyp. 1, Teksty (folklor), M.1963

Idem, *Indoiranskiye dialekty Gissarskoi doliny (Indiiskii dialekt parya. Goyory I argo Tajikoyazhichnikh etnograficheskikh grupp),".* Materialy I issledovaniya. Avtoref. Dokt. Diss., Leningrad, 1967

Idem, "Legenda o sheikhe Shamsi Tabrizi" in *Ellinisticheski Bliizhnii Vostok. Vizantiya i Iran, M. 1967*

Idem, "Nauchnaya kommandirovka v dolinu Gissara I Surkhan Darya" in *Sovetskkaya Etnografiya.* 1966, No.4

Idem, "Novyye svedeniya o sekretnikh yazykakh Srednei Azii (1). Etnograficheskaya gruppa "Kabol" v Kulbe I yee argo" in *KCINA,* XL, Yazykoznaniye, M., 1961.

Idem, "Novyye svedeniya o sekretnykh yazykakh (argo) Srednei Azii (II). Materialy dlya izucheniya argo etnograficheskoi gruppy jugi (Gissarskaya dolina" in *Iranskaya filologiya.* T*rudy nauchnoi konferentsii po iranskoi filolology* (24-27 yanvarya 1962g.), LGU, 1964

Idem, " Predvaritelnoye soobsheniya ob obnaruzhennom v srednei Azii indiiskom dialekte "in *Sovetskoye Vostokoyvedeniye,* 1956, No.4

Dictionaries, Encyclopaedia, etc.

The Encyclopaedia of Islam, Vol. 1, London-Leyden, 1913

H.A. Rose, *Glossary of the Tribles and Castes of the Punjab and the North-West Frontier Province Based on the Census Report for the Punjab, 1883* and the Census Report for the Punjab, 1882. Lahore, Vol. I, 1919, Vol. II, 1911, Vol. III, 1914

Hobson-Jobson, *A Glossary of Coloquial Anglo-Indian Words and Phrases, and of Kindred Terms* by Henry Yule and A.C. Burnell, London, 1903

B.V. Miller, *Persidsko-russkii slovar*, Moscow, 1950

R.L. Turner, *A Comparative Dictionary of the Indo-Aryan Languages*, London, 1966.

Linguistic Survey of India, Vol. XI, Calcutta, 1922

Archives Consulted
[1] National Archives of India, New Delhi
[2] Punjab State Achives, Patiala

Archives Consulted in the Countries formerly part of the USSR
[1] Arkhiv Vnesshnyi Politiki Rossii
[2] Leningradskoy otdeleniye Instituta Narodov Azii (Akademiya Nayk, USSR)
[3] Tsentralnyi Gosudarstvenyi Arkhiv, USSR
[4] Tsentralnyi Gosudarstvenyi Arkhiv Uzbekistan SSR
[5] Tsentralnyi Gosudarstvenyi Vneshnii Istorichreskii Arkhiv

Journals and Newspapers Consulted

Journals
(I) in Russian
Istoria SSSR
Narody Azii I Afriki
Sovietskaya Etnografiya
Ruskii Anthropologicheskii Zhurnal
Sovetskoye Vostokovedeniye
Voprosy Istorii
(II) English
Central Asian Review
Journal of the Bombay Branch of Royal Asiatic Society, *New Series*
Journal of the Central Asian Society
The Journal of Central Asian Studies, *Srinagar*
Fortnightly Review

Bibliography

Newspapers (in Russian)
Moskovskie Vedomosti, 1889
Novoye Vremya, 1879
Prosveshcheniye, Tashkent
Russkii Vestnik
Turkestanskii Kurier, 1908

In Uzbek
Turkiston Viloytining Gazeti, 1889

Index

A. Ya. Elifanov associate of an Indian merchant 84

A.E. Snesarev 65

A.F. Gubarevich-Radobylskii on Indian trade with Kashgar 62

A.I. Vilkins ethnographer 150

Abdalees 29

Abdul Abbas Muhammad author 10

Abdul Hamid of Peshawar 108

Abdul Majid merchant of Peshawar in Samarkand 108

Abdul Rahman Khan, Russian agent 114

Abdul Shahid, Uzbek envoy to Mughals 4

Abdul Wahab Russian emissary in Kashmir 114

Abdulla Paracha of Rawalpindi in Central Asia 116

Abdullah Khan II, his conquests 7

Abdullah Multani owned houses in Samarkand 9

Abdur Razzak, envoy of Herat 4

Abdur Rahman Khan fugitive Afghan Amir 115, 119

Abul Fazl chronicler 2

advanced money to government in Afghanistan 29

Afanasi Nikitin Russian traveller to India 4, 44

Afganistan 61

afgany (afagno) used for Indian paria 145

Afghan 151

Afghan Amir his meeting with Ishan of Kokand 112

Afghan Amir Abdul Rahman Khan 61, 125

Afghan mercantile groups 22

Afghan tribe 21

Afghanistan 2, 20-30, 35-37, 45, 46, 48, 53, 59, 61, 62, 66, 69, 100, 105, 110, 112, 149, 153

Afghans 9, 28, 34, 46, 53, 55, 102, 103, 123

Afgono name of Indian paria 139, 145

afgono-yi nosfurus (nospurus) 145

Afgono-yi siyorul (siyopust) 145

Africa 1

agents, Russian to Bukhare 13

Agra 122

agriculture, Indians in Central Asia engaged in 67, 140

Ahmed Shah Abdalee 28, 29

Ahmedabad 7

Aini on Indian moneylenders 66

Ajmer 122

Ak Mesjid seized by Russians 122

Akbar 3

Akbar's reign 59

Aksakal chief of Indians in Central Asia 79

Aksu visited by Rafailov 35, 49; road from Kashmir to 50

Aktan mountain towards Ladakh 51

Akub-Sheikh Nurkhanov Indian from

Burma 100
Burnes 61, 104, 106; visit to Bukhara 61
business intelligence 23
business of banking 29
buzkasi (game) 142

C.H. Ellis 128
C.I. Pazukhin 13
Cabul 24, 25, 35, 60 (see Kabul)
Cafila (Kafila) 31, 32
Calcutta 34, 102, 122; by sea 102
California 129
camels from Samarkand 6; in Kandahar 11
capital 24
capitalism 76
Capt. James Abbott 104
Capt. Montgomerie trainer of Indian explorers 106
Captain Pottinger on trade with Central Asia 103
Caravan(s) 4, 5, 26, 48, 49, 55; route(s) to Kabul and Central Asia 20, 59; trade of India 4, 11, 76
Caravan-serai(s) for Hindus in Tashkent and Bukhara 9, 24, 34, 80, 89, 104; in Herat 24
carpets from Turkistan 6, 37
cásgarak of paria 149
Cashan 25
Caspian 45; fire temple 104
Caspian Sea 2, 5, 11, 26, 29, 46, 63, 64
castes and tribes of India 147
Catechism taught in Central Asia 92
Caucasus 46; region 28
causes of rivalry between Russians and British 99
cavalry 53
Census of population 77
Central Asia 3, 4, 6, 7, 9, 13, 14, 20-25, 26, 28, 32, 35-38, 47, 56, 59,

60-68, 76, 77, 92, 99-101, 103-112, 123; trade centre, 45
Central Asia region 32
Central Asian(s) 1, 6, 11, 14, 65, 99, 139; Affairs 111; cities 9, 13, 28, 32; Commercial Bank 69; horses 6; Khanates 46, 47, 71, 79, 106, 124; markets 5, 32, 63 ,103; merchants coming to India 37; politics 12; press 66; Republics 77; route via Kazakh Steppe 46; rulers 28; soil 24; trade with India 61, 65
Central State Archives of Military History of U.S.S.R. 121
Chachgarak name of paria 149
'Changar'(s) used for paria 146, 147, 152
Chardjui, Indian druggists in, 70
Chenab river in the Punjab 14
Cherkin, Russian Consul in Bombay 122
Cherno Yar in Russia 12
Khernayer, Russian General 107, 108, 120
Chetram Mingraj, India book binder in Tashkent 70
Childas father of Febdas in Bukhara 95
China 3, 4, 9, 59, 64, 104, 114
China stuff in Central Asia 35
Chinese 26, 63; empire 3; Turkistan 46,59; held territory 48
Chinese-ruled Eastern Turkistan 46
chintz(s) imported in Central Asia from India 31, 35, 60, 101, 109
Chiragchi town in Bukhara 107
Chirchick town in Bukhara 107
chistoni name of paria 150
Chit-i-Purband a variety of textile in Samarkand 8
Chitral 62
Chittor visited by Amirov 122
Christian, an Indian becomes 12

Index

Index

Index

Morgensterne Norwegian linguist 152
mortgage by Indians for advancing loans 66
Moscow 2, 11, 33, 44, 94, 100, 133
Mughal 6, 45; chronicles 12; control 10; Emperor 109; Jahangir 10; Empire 13, 14; history 2; period 2, 14; power 37; rule 19, 27; ruler 12
Mughal soliders 5
Mughals 7, 9, 12, 19, 27, 28, 59
Muhammad Yusuf Munshi author 76
Muhammad Yusuf Kasimov Russian envoy in Kabul 13
Muhammadan Chuhra in Punjab 148
Muhammed Niaz news writer 107
Muhsin Khwaja received gift from Jahangir 10
Mukhsoom Uzbek merchant in Bukhara 103
Mukim-Khanskaya Istoriya Persian chronicle 76
Mulla Hussain sent to Khiva by British 104
Mulla Iwaz Muhammad British Agent 107
Mulla Mohammed Amin at Kunduz 100
Mulla Painda Multani in Samarkand 8, 10
Mullah Hussain son of Mulla Painda 8
Mullah Ikram Tajik from Kattakurgan 113, 115
Multan 3, 9, 20, 21, 23, 31, 32, 37, 59, 77, 122
Multan imported silk from Bengal, Kashmir, China, 31
Multanis (Multani) 2, 20, 21, 23, 26, 31
murders 67
Murshidabad in Bengal 122
musalli name of paria 144, 149
Mushyamal Himanmalev Indian knew Uzbek 91

Muslim 21; Indian traders 2, 26, 81; population 2, 21; surveyor 103; theology and law 101
Muslims 9, 22, 53, 56, 112
Muslims and non-Muslims 27
muslin 31, 62, 63, 81, 82; Dacca 60
mussali name of paria 148
Mustafin from Kashmir knew Uzbek 91
Muzdaban mountain of snow 51
Mysore in India 46

N. Khanykov Russian traveller to Central Asia 61
N.A. Ivanov cooperated with an Indian 69
N.P. Rumyantsev Foreign Minister of Russia 49
Nadir Saferov Tatar came to India with goods 34
Nadir Shah ruler of Iran 28, 33, 46
Nadir Shah's assassination 28
Nagore in India 122
Naib Ressaldar in Indian army 112
Namangan (Nemangan) in Central Asia 70, 79
Namdhari (Kuka) Sikhs 120; see Kukas
Namdhari envoy met Kanfmann 121
Nana Saheb 116
Napoleon Bonaparte (Napoleon) 45, 100
Naqshabandi Khwaja, his dead body wrapped with Kashmiri shawl 32
Naqshbandi order in Central Asia 10
nas 145
National Archives of India 108, 122
national bourgeoisie of India 76
native merchants 111; tongue 141
Nawab of Lucknow 121
Nazar Kul former Governor of Namagan 112

Index

rail linking Central Asia and India 65; linking India and Russia 66

raisins imported into India 6

Rajaori in Kashmir 113

Rajasthan 20

Rajput 23

Ram Chandra (Tora) (Balaji), nephew of Nana Saheb, friendship with Russian scholars, reconnaissance of Oxus river 94, 116

Ram Das Kishnu Indian in Central Asia 70

Ram Singh Shikarpuri moneylender 115

Rampur in Uttar Pradesh 116

Ranjit Singh 50 (see Maharaja Ranjit Singh)

rate of exchange on Bills of Exchange 28

Rauzat-ur Rizawan va hadikat al-gilman Persian chronicle 10

Ravi river in Panjab 21

raw silk imported in India 32, 36

Rawalpindi district 112, 116

Rawlinson author 105

Razzak Abdur chronicler 4

reconnaissance of Oxus river 94

red chillies imported into Central Asia 32

Red Sea ports 2

regular trade with India 37

religious history 92; preachers 2

reports of Russian merchants 47

Republic of Uzbekistan 19

resident Indians in Central Asia 2

restrictions imposed by Russian authorities 71

return of Rabbani to India 108

returned to India, moneylenders 68

Reuben, Jew in Central Asia 113

revolt of tribes 62

Reza Ali Indian in Samarkand 109

rich bankers 30

Ridgeway's papers in National Archives of India 125

rituals performed by Indians in Central Asia 88

rivalry between Russia and British in India 100

robbed Indian caravan on way to Central Asia 5

Robert Steel British traveller 11

route 32, 46, 47, 62

route through Kabul 62

route (routes) to India 45, 54, 65

route to India via Central Asian Khanates 46

Roy M.N., Indian revolutionary 133

royal buildings, Indian slaves to work on 10

Rugs brought to Multan 37

ruler of Kashmir 54, 55, 102; Tibet 49; 'Tibet' 50

Rumyantsev Russian Foreign Minister 48

Russia 5, 11, 22, 34, 45, 46, 49, 51, 55, 60, 63, 65, 66, 96, 101, 102, 105, 109, 111, 113

Russian 1, 4, 26, 33, 38, 44, 101, 110, 143; administration of Samarkand 63, 108; advance(s) 119, 56; agent 105; annexation 119; Army 108; attempt to establish contact with Kashmir 102; authorities 32, 34, 45, 79, 92, 113, 114; authors 67; bourgeoisie 63, 67; boxes 65; capital 49; ceramics 71; children 93; cities 37; cloth 65; colonial officials 80; commodities 62; conquest 119; Consul(s) 111, 122; Consul-General in Bombay 65; Consulate 65; contacts 44; designs on Central Asia 99; doctors in Central Asia 93; Emperor Tsar Alexander I 101; Empress

Contributors

Devendra Kaushik, presently the Chairman of the Executive Council of Maulana Abul Kalam Azad Institute of Asian Studies, Calcutta retired as a Professor from the Jawaharlal Nehru University. He has lived in Tashkent and Moscow for several years and has authored a number of books on Central Asia and the Soviet Union. He is a known expert on Soviet and Russian affairs.

Surendra Gopal, retired Professor of History, Patna University, has published a series of articles on Indian diaspora in Iran, Russia and Central Asia from the XVI Century to the XX Century. He has also published a book and several research papers on India's maritime trade in medieval times.

G.L. Dmitriyev was a prominent historian based in Tashkent where he worked extensively in the archives of the Tsarist and Soviet times and on the basis of data collected wrote a doctoral dissertation on the activities of the immigrant Indian community during the second half of the nineteenth and early twentieth centuries.

Iosif Mikhailovich Oranskii (03.05.1923-16.05.1977), a linguist by profession worked from 1959 to 1977 in the Leningrad branch of the Institute of Oriental Studies, ANSSR. He carried field work in Tajikistan and discovered a community of immigrant Indians, who spoke in a language similar to that of Panjabi and Rajasthani.